1/74

TOMA
The Compassionate Cop

Dave the detective, on the left, with actor Tony Musante, star in the television series *Toma*.

TOMA
The Compassionate Cop

by

David Toma with Michael Brett

G. P. PUTNAM'S SONS
New York

SBN: 399-11277-4

Library of Congress Catalog Card Number: 73-87178

Printed in the United States of America

For Patricia, of course, and our children, Jimmy, Patty Ann, Donna and Janice.

In memoriam, David Toma, Jr.

Illustrations will be found following page 135.

We gratefully acknowledge the help and cooperation given by Mayor Kenneth A. Gibson, Police Director Domenick A. Spina, Chief of Police Anthony Barres, Inspector Irving J. Moore, Inspector Charles Zizza, Captain Robert Parkinson, Captain Thomas O'Reilly, Lieutenant Thomas E. Dougherty, Detective Anthony Nicosia, and the detectives and police officers of Newark and the state of New Jersey.

And a special thanks for Ruth Brett's critical eye.

TOMA

The Compassionate Cop

CHAPTER ONE

It seemed that the whores and pimps of Newark and various muggers, perverts and assassins were getting out of hand. There were numerous complaints from the victims who complained bitterly about the lack of protection. They were unfortunate, but not as unfortunate as Jerry Ledtke, a middle-aged businessman who'd come to Newark for action. He was seen entering an abandoned building on the heels of a prostitute, and shortly thereafter Ledtke had been mugged in her third-story room and thrown out of a window to the concrete below, where he instantly died.

As a result, the newspapers had run front-page editorials requesting more police protection for the good citizen and quoting statistics about how crime was increasing and the venereal disease rate was at an all-time high and how the good citizens and taxpayers could no longer walk the streets of Newark without getting their heads bashed in. But there was nothing in the editorials about straightening the Johns out, about telling them that if they didn't seek out the whores, then the whores wouldn't be there and they wouldn't get their heads bashed. So how do you change human nature? There were always going to be prostitutes, and there were always going to be Johns. It was a fact of life.

Try charging the trick with soliciting and book the hooker as a material witness and see what happens. I charged a guy like that once, and I had every political hack in Essex County jumping down my throat and interceding on his behalf. Like that, you can even get a little pressure from your superiors. I recall Lieutenant Vince Kendricks saying, "Come on, Dave, what the hell you trying to do, change human nature? The guy is out looking for a piece. So what? What are you going to do, change the rules or something?"

"Why not?" I said. "If the rules need changing, then why not change them?"

Kendricks said, "The guy is a family man. He's got kids. You'll ruin the guy's home life." And then he growled something about some politician who was putting pressure on him and that he didn't need it.

So it ended right then and there. Everybody walked away from it.

The murder was an altogether different story and not dismissed as lightly. Domenick "Dick" Spina, the police director, issued a direct order that he wanted the area cleaned up. "Get them the hell out of there. The street is lousy with whores, pimps, perverts, junkies and muggers. I mean it. Get rid of them."

So the requests had gone on down from the captain to the lieutenant to the sergeant, and action was being taken. We were putting heat on the street.

These were the facts that were responsible for putting me on the street at three o'clock on a Saturday morning in the dead of winter.

My name is David Toma. I'm forty years old, and I'm a detective attached to the Bureau of Investigation which is the department that handles gambling, narcotics and vice in Newark. My partner was a rookie named Nick Ragone. Homicide had been given the murder, and the Bureau of Investigation had been told to put pressure on the prostitutes. The prostitutes knew there was heat on the street, and they were a little more cautious than what was their usual custom. As a result, we'd been driving around for the last three hours keeping the area under surveillance. I didn't have anything to say to the rookie. Having him assigned to me could be a headache. There's nothing reassuring about having a rookie for your partner. I've got a bad back, and sitting in the car in one position had intensified the pain. It didn't make for a feeling of well-being.

Ledtke's death had raised a large hue and cry. He'd been a respected, affluent member of his community and the owner of a large discount beauty supply chain. There were those who questioned Ledtke's wisdom in seeking out a prostitute in a particularly dangerous area. They reasoned, that if Ledtke wanted to play around, he could have afforded a mistress, a girlfriend or even a call girl with whom he would have entertained a greater degree of personal safety.

Instead, Jerry Ledtke had entered a grimy abandoned building with a streetwalker to a shabby third-story room, where he had been assaulted and thrown to his death. It was hardly an intelligent, predictable, or even sane act for an informed, knowledgeable type like Jerry Ledtke. You can become cynical. I felt sorrow for Ledtke's widow and his three children. She had problems; Jerry no longer had any.

We circled the block at High Street and Springfield Avenue and watched a procession of cars driven by white men attempting to pick up black prostitutes. Some of the drivers pulled over to the curb; others double parked and signaled or waited for the prostitutes to approach. It could be a game of Russian roulette. He picks her up, and she takes him up to some cruddy apartment, and he walks away in one piece. Lucky. Or maybe there are some guys waiting for him in her place and he never gets out of there alive. They roll him, and maybe there's a guy up there who thinks nothing of killing Paddy. "Shit, I ain't taking any chance that this motherfucker is ever going to pick me out of any motherfuckin' lineup someday." And so it's all over. And maybe you find the guy's legs over on one of those lots in the Central Ward that looks like Hiroshima in World War II. And maybe that's all you ever find of him. I've seen too much of that.

The light rain became a sudden torrent, and some of the prostitutes jumped into the waiting cars. Others darted to the shelter of hallways. I pulled over, parked and turned the ignition off to wait out the downpour.

Ragone was a nice-looking kid about twenty-three. He was a big, powerful guy. I'd been told that he'd been an outstanding college football tackle. He looked as though he could handle himself. Despite it, his presence didn't put me at ease. I'm never completely at ease with a rookie who's out with me because I don't know how he's going to react if trouble starts. He's been through the Police Academy, and he's been taught everything they can teach him. But this driving around in the middle of a dark night is a different ball game, and you meet very few con men, extortionists, pimps, prostitutes, knifers, larcenists, arsonists, ax murderers, cop haters and cop killers at the Police Academy. There might be an ordinary-looking guy ambling around out there who's a fugitive from the law in a couple of states for murder. Ask him who he is and he pulls a gun and starts blasting. He has to get away, and what has he got to lose by killing?

So you take a reasonably intelligent man like Ragone, and it figures that he's a little excited, apprehensive and afraid. In the doorways he can see black males who know that he's whitey cruising around looking for a black woman like the rest of the jokers hunting black hookers. Ragone sees them in the doorways and the taverns, and he sees the hate and contempt in their eyes.

They blame the whites for their misery, and Ragone knows it. It's Ragone's first assignment, and he doesn't know what to expect. I'm on the force for seventeen years, and in my mind I know I'm good at my job. I know what I'm doing. I've got the credentials to back it up. I've been responsible directly and indirectly for more than 9,000 arrests, and there's a 98 percent conviction record that goes along with it. And yet I don't really know what to expect on the street. I'm not going to take a backward step at this point and attempt to come across as a shy, modest, shrinking-violet-type fellow. I believe in myself, and I know that I couldn't have made my record without having a good-sized ego.

The rain lightened, and the whores began to leave their places of shelter. They were on the street again. Out of the corner of my eye I observed that Ragone appeared on edge.

"Here we go," he said. "The hump marketplace is open for business."

"Before we start fishing for hookers, let's go over what I've already told you, so that when we make a pinch we don't come up looking foolish and the pinch stands up when it gets into court."

Ragone grinned. "I got it. She's got to do the soliciting. She's got to make the offer. A piece of tail for money."

I nodded. "Basically that's the way it has to be. It has to be more than her offering you a good time in her pad. In court that could mean that she's charging you twenty bucks for the privilege of watching the late-late show on her television set or a friendly game of checkers. It can mean anything. If she doesn't lay it all out on the line nice and clear for you, then you go to her apartment. When she disrobes and reveals herself to you and asks you for the money, then you've got a good pinch. She doesn't have to ask you for the money at that point. You've still got a good pinch, but in all cases they'll ask you for the money right then and there, and that's when you tell her that she's under arrest. Tonight we play it by ear. You watch and you don't do anything on your own."

"It doesn't sound that tough. You sure that you don't want me to go ahead and try it? The lieutenant said something about needing more arrests for the monthly quota," Ragone said with a faint smile.

He irritated me. He was a rookie who already had all the answers. My second thought was that it was false bravado. I explained, "The hooker has run into more vice cops than you've run into hookers. You say the wrong thing or make the wrong move and she'll spot you. It can happen in her room, and if she starts yelling, you might have all kinds of guys coming to her aid. They can be real mean types. They'd think nothing of cutting you up. You play it my way."

"Whatever you say," Ragone said. "You're the boss."

I handed him my gun and shield, and he placed them on the floor under the front seat. When I left my car, Ragone slid over behind the wheel. "Keep your eyes on me," I said, "and just stay with the car. If I get a bite, I'll be back."

I walked away from the car as though I was a little smashed

along a darkened littered sidewalk for about fifty feet and passed an abandoned burned-out wooden frame house. The stench of garbage filled my nostrils. I listened for the sounds of danger. A footstep out there in the darkness could mean a two-legged animal trying to overtake you stealthily with a knife in his hand. Perhaps a mugger or a homicidal maniac. They don't know that you're a cop. They're out there and you know it. Newark had 160 homicides last year. In a city of 380,000 that's a lot of dead people. And the thought comes to you that you've got to be a little crazy to put your life on the line trying to apprehend some prostitute.

There was a rustling sound in front of me, and a huge rat disengaged himself from a pile of garbage and scurried to a position on the sidewalk facing me not more than five feet away. I froze. His red eyes stared at me, sizing me up as though he were contemplating the prospect of gnawing on my leg. I hate rats because I fear them. It goes all the way back to my childhood, and thinking about them can make me ill.

The street was dark. Most of the streetlamps were broken. I almost missed the girl. There was a sharp hissing sound from a darkened doorway and a woman's voice, "Hey, baby, how about a little fun?"

I didn't know if she was alone. I lit a match and in the flickering light caught a glimpse of a young black woman. She wore an Afro, short coat, short skirt and knee-high boots. She was dark and tall, and her face was handsome. I thought that she was a lot of woman to be peddling her ass to some crud whose guts she hated.

I said, "Where are we going, and what's it going to be?"

The match went out. She stared at me in the darkness. "Baby, you don't look like a cop, but you just might be and I ain't taking any chances."

She hadn't recognized me as a cop, and I'd never seen her

before either. It was time for act one, scene one. "Look," I said. "I just came down here looking for some ass. I don't need a fucking third degree. If a man wants something like that, he don't have to explain it."

"I heard that line of shit from cops before, and the first thing they're pulling their badge and telling me that I'm under arrest. Fuck that. I don't feel right about you."

I tried a different approach. "Listen, I got busted three weeks ago. I don't need your shit. You see me arguing price with you? What the fuck you mean calling me a cop? You got any problems, girl, they're your problems. I don't need your problems, so take a walk. I'll get somebody who knows what the hell she's doing. I got a feeling we start making it and you're not going to know what the fuck you're doing anyway."

She drew on her cigarette. She was smiling. "Hell, I guess you're all right. It's going to cost you twenty dollars and five dollars for the room."

"Okay, but what's all this about five dollars for the room?" I asked with a touch of indignation.

"Well, honey, I got rent to pay for the privilege of laying my ass down on the mattress."

More likely she'd be left with only five dollars after her pimp took his cut. "Why didn't you come right out with it and say that you wanted twenty-five?" I said in a softer tone. Toma the great, putting a whore at ease. Listen to yourself doing it and maybe you laugh at yourself while feeling a little pity for the prostitute.

"If you like, you can pay me now, baby," she said hopefully.

"Come on," I said, laughing. "You'd probably break the world's speed record running with all that money."

She laughed aloud. "Shee-it. You really believe that? Honey, I'm going to change you. I finish up with you, you going to be a changed man. I French and I got the best pussy in all of Newark. My little pussy practically talks to you."

It was a direct reference to pussy power. I thought of Jerry Ledtke, who had been killed by it. I had enough on her right now to make the collar. She'd made the offer and quoted a price. But guys were getting killed in those pads, and there were orders to clean up the street. There was a chance that she could lead me to bigger game. "Okay, where do we go?"

"It's not far. Stay back about half a block. Just follow me."

I gave her the distance she'd requested. Under the dim streetlights her good legs moved ahead quickly. Business was business, and the sooner she got this trick's money, the sooner she'd be able to get on with her trade. I glanced back and saw Ragone in the car. I'd instructed him not to follow us because of the chance that she might have her pimp lurking around waiting to spot a tail. It was two blocks straight ahead through the cold deserted street and then a turn to the right into an alley. It was narrow, littered with discarded tires, refrigerators, trash and the stench of something that had died long ago.

Up ahead I could see her threading her way through the debris. She made a turn to the left and disappeared. An ancient gin-soaked hooker in a ratty fur coat loomed up before me. She whispered, "Wanta get laid?"

"Tomorrow," I said. "When there's a full moon."

"Well, fuck you," she replied and stalked off to disappear into the shadows whence she had come.

I laughed quietly at our performances. Go ahead, start taking this action lightly. You're walking through all this darkness, and maybe when you reach the corner, somebody swings a two-by-four across your head and it's all over. Take the job for granted. Get a little careless, and maybe you don't sleep in your own bed anymore.

The building on my right was completely blacked out. On the left, dim light behind drawn shades filtered down. Then there was total darkness. I stood perfectly still, waited for my eyes to adjust and listened for the sound of movement.

There was a faint glow from her cigarette about fifteen feet away to the left. "Over here," she said. "What you waiting for?"

I realized that she was standing in an open doorway and made my way over there. The stench of urine and decay was overpowering. Her hand reached out and took my arm. It was possible that there was somebody waiting for me in that small place with a gun, knife or club. There could be more than one man. You're in the business, you've seen it. You think of your own vulnerability.

I drew my arm away and struck a match. There was no objection from her, no fear of any possible trouble. The darkened stinking hallways were her bailiwick. She was completely at ease, just getting ready to pull another trick. Midway down the corridor she rapped three times lightly. The door was opened by a massive form. He was black, solely illuminated by a flickering candle on a table in the corner of the room. He was big enough to give three cops trouble. He made a very careful appraisal, then stepped aside as we went in. I was cautious, never taking my eyes off him. She led me across the room to a door that was slightly ajar. From the room itself came the odor of marijuana smoke, like burning rope, and the unmistakable sounds of creaking bedsprings and muffled grunting sounds.

The prostitute laughed. "Don't pay any attention to what's going on," she said, and pushed at the door.

It was a small room except for a mattress on the floor. There were four nude people on it. A couple slept on one side.

Oblivious to the sleeping pair, another couple pumped away. There was a momentary pause when they became aware of us, but they made no effort to disentangle. The man glanced back over his shoulder, and the girl glared. She grumbled, "Mae, why the fuck don't you knock or something?"

I thought she had a valid complaint.

It was a big railroad apartment with the rooms all in line. We made our way to the next room. There was a sharp odor of kerosene. Two men sat at a table; one was black and the other white with tattooed arms and a goatee. On a filthy bed there was a very young nude black girl asleep. The legs of the bed rested in kerosene-filled cans as a deterrent to an army of roaches darting across the floor. A bloodstained cotton gauze tourniquet and a fire-blackened spoon were on the floor near where she slept. Her thin arms were covered with festering sores. I felt myself slipping into depression. The girl was like so much dead meat, as though something had already killed her. It brought anger, and with anger cool decisions are lost. I pushed it out of my mind.

The two men sitting impassively in the corner of the room bothered me. It was a bad time to be without a gun. Sometimes it can be easy to talk your way into a situation and much more difficult to worm your way out of it. It wasn't just a whore's pad into which I had wandered. It was a shooting gallery, and it figured that there were drugs stashed somewhere. If the two men in the room made me out to be the "man," then I was going to have my hands full. I'd seen sharks like them on a hundred darkened streets waiting patiently for the right victim to come along. They could be very capable at the business of putting somebody away for good.

We went into the kitchen, where there was light. Mae grinned at me. "Sit down. I'm just going to make sure that you

21

ain't carrying anything." She removed her coat and then her dress and stood close. She patted me down proficiently searching for gun, cuffs, shield, anything that might give her a clue that I was a cop.

"What the hell you looking for?" I said angrily. If I antagonized her, then the hell with it. At this point I had come to the conclusion that the whole business stank and that maybe I was in over my head. I didn't like the setup. The three guys in the apartment stank, and the young girl stretched out half-dead, that stank, the whore patting me down stank, the roaches stank, and being unarmed stank. My back-up man was a rookie, and that stank too.

Satisfied that I was clean, she rested her hand over my thigh and with one quick motion unzipped my fly.

"Well"—Mae smiled—"you ain't going to do anything with that, in the condition it's in."

Her hand slid behind her back and undid the snap that held her bra in place and with one quick movement pulled a strap over her shoulder and revealed a beautifully shaped breast. She loosened her bra from the other shoulder and dropped it on the kitchen table.

Maybe I was supposed to say, "What a great pair, or what are we waiting for, or how do we get to the nearest bedroom?" I said nothing. I kept thinking about three mean-looking guys. The odds were all wrong. I wanted out. I began to get up.

"Billy," she called.

She was leaning over me and I got up so quickly I sent her sprawling.

"Billy! Billy!" she screamed.

There was an onrush of pounding feet from the other rooms. There was a window in the farthest room of the apartment that had a sheet of plywood nailed over it. It would have taken too much time to kick it loose. For weapons there was a sagging bed and a three-legged chair next to it. Worn linoleum covered the floor. Lathe showed through the ceiling. It was a mean, ugly little cubicle, a sad place to die.

"Now just come out of there, you son of a bitch," Billy said. He was the one who had let us into the apartment.

Maybe I could come out swinging the chair, or maybe I could get lucky, or maybe I could have tried the Lord's Prayer. I came out with my hands raised and my fingers spread wide.

Billy held a kitchen knife. One of his partners held a .45, and the other, the goateed one, brandished an open switchblade.

Billy said, "He giving you trouble, Mae?"

"He ain't shit. I been messing with him for five minutes and he can't do nothing. He's a fuckin' fag."

"Sit down on that chair before I cut your head off," Billy said, waving the kitchen knife, demonstrating how he was going to do it.

I sat, and he held the knife at my throat. An insane giggling came from the man with the goatee. "Let's cut his fuckin' head off."

"Yeah, I might do that, Ralph," Billy said quietly.

My voice came out in a thin whisper. "You guys had me scared. I came in and there were three of you and I didn't know what to expect. I saw all those roaches on the floor and I just couldn't get it up. That's all. Nobody's trying to do her out of the money." The words were spoken so quickly they ran into each other. They ended in a whine. I wouldn't risk an indignant tone.

"How much money you got?" the short one said.

Their plan would be to take my money and kill me. It was as cut-and-dried as that. Knock him off, drag him into an abandoned basement, dig a shallow grave and cover him with debris. Or why bother at all? Who the hell is going to come looking for him in an abandoned basement in Newark? And how's anybody going to trace the killing?

The human mind becomes inventive when survival is at stake. "There's more than what I just told you. I didn't come down here by myself tonight. There's another guy with me, and he's got me nervous. He's the guy who brought me down here." The words were coming quickly. "We were sitting in the car, and he got out and started to talk to some queers, and they started arguing in the street, calling each other names, and when he came back to the car, I asked him what that was all about. He said that he was only kidding, and that he just wanted to have some fun with fags." You talk, and you know that if you talk, you're still alive. "Anyway, I left him and went out by myself, but he's got me worried because I left my money with him, and that ain't helping me make it with her," I said, glancing at Mae. "How am I going to get it up when I keep thinking about this guy in the car with my money?"

"You mean you ain't got any money on you now?" the goateed one said ominously.

"Hell, yeah, I got the money. I got fifty dollars on me, but I left four hundred and fifty dollars with him in the car. I didn't want to carry that around with me." They would kill me for fifty dollars, but they might delay it while trying for a larger amount.

The pressure of the knife at my throat lessened slightly, and I caught the tiny flicker of interest in his eyes.

"I told you that he's a jerk. He is supposed to wait in the car until I come back. But I keep thinking that he's going to find himself some trouble, and maybe they'll roll him. He's carrying my money on him." I glanced at Mae and smiled. "Man, she's really something. I really wanted to give it to her."

Billy smiled and removed the knife from my throat. "She's the best ass in town."

And now the three of them were smiling, thinking of $450 plus $50, already counting it and dividing it up. You become what you do. You deal with the pimps, whores, gamblers and junkies long enough and you learn to think like them. Why should they settle for $50 when there was a possible $500 score? Greed had them on the hook. It was going to take a little more talk, and maybe I was going to con my way out of here.

We all heard somebody trying the door.

"Dave, Dave, you in there?"

I recognized Ragone's voice. In the stillness it sounded as though he were using a bullhorn. Everybody froze. The knife came back to my throat again, and the handgun came up, pointing at my head. My head felt cold. It was a ripe time for a killing. "It's my friend," I blurted. "He must be looking for me." I had no idea how Ragone had found the apartment.

It was a different ball game, and I wasn't sure how it should be played. There were too many ifs to consider. Ragone could be standing behind the door with a gun in his hand or in his belt or taped on his leg. I wanted him unarmed. If he came barging through the door, somebody was going to get hurt.

Billy opened a kitchen drawer and calmly removed a .38. "You open the door. If your friend got anybody with him or something goes wrong, you're dead."

You keep it cool when it's like that. I tried grinning. "Don't go scaring the shit out of him. I know he's just looking to get laid, so don't go scaring the shit out of him."

He motioned me to walk to the door and followed with the muzzle of the gun against my back. He stood next to me behind the door as I opened it. Ragone was out there with a flashlight. He could see only me. The others had positioned themselves out of sight.

"What the hell you doing?" Ragone said. "You told me you were going to come back if you found something." He leered at me. "You got a couple of broads in there, right?" He was no fool, he sensed that I wasn't alone.

Billy stepped out from behind the door and said, "Get in here."

Ragone paled perceptively and came in. "What? What the hell is this?"

I said, "You got my money on you?"

He gave me a blank stare.

"You dumb son of a bitch. You mean you left four hundred and fifty dollars in the car? In this neighborhood? You out of your fuckin' mind?" I had been nervous as hell when the door was opened, but now, talking to him, I could actually feel myself calming down. I turned to Billy. "Would you believe that he's so stupid?"

Ragone caught on instantly. "Nobody's going to bother the car. Who the hell is going to bother it?" he said. "If you want, I'll go down and get the dough. I didn't want to carry it on me."

I turned to Billy. "Listen, I'll go for it myself."

Mae screamed, "He ain't going anywhere. I been playing with him, and I'm half undressed and I ain't seen a fuckin' dime."

Billy stared at me. "She's right," he said.

I reached into my pocket and handed him $50. "Listen, I really want to get laid, and I know I can't do it while I'm worrying about somebody stealing my money." I pointed to the money in his hand. "You just make sure nobody steals that fifty. And there's ten dollars in it for you." I smiled at Mae. "She gets forty."

"What about me?" Ragone said. "Where the hell do I come in?" He looked at Mae. "I'm no orphan."

"Come on in the other room," Mae said.

Ragone patted his pocket. "I guess you want to get paid first."

She stared at him in disbelief. "You bet I do. You some kind of dumb ass-hole?"

"I left my wallet in the car," Ragone said. "I didn't want to take any chances of getting mugged in the street."

"Sheeit," said the bearded one.

Billy looked us over deliberately. "You don't come back and you're out fifty dollars and you ain't even had a hand job for it." Somewhere in back of his eyes there was a cash register that was ringing up $450. He already had $50 and he thought he was talking to two squares who might possibly return. He had nothing to lose by letting us go. I doubted that he'd follow us to try for a hit on the street.

Ragone and I started for the door.

"Don't be all night," Mae said. "I got to make me some coin." Now she was also part of the act.

"Just keep that thing warm," I said. "We'll be back in less than ten minutes."

"Don't flash that light around out there in the alley," Billy warned Ragone as we were leaving.

On the street I felt a peculiar letdown. We weren't through, but the immediate crisis had passed. It had left my stomach knotted.

"Let's get the guns," I said. We ran toward the car. I had mixed emotions regarding Ragone. He hadn't played it the way I'd told him. He hadn't waited for me to return. He'd left the car with our guns and shields unprotected. In this neighborhood one could expect the car to be stolen. He'd come looking for me without his gun. That was a mistake on the face of it, and yet if he had had a gun in his hand when I opened the door, just as sure as I was alive recalling it, Billy would have shot me. You can rehash a thing like that for hours and never come up with the way it should have been played. It could have been a combination of luck and stupidity, or it could have been that Ragone had acted the way he did because he was green. Meanwhile, we were both alive and you don't question what might have been.

We scrambled into the car, and I got the .38 and the .32 and placed them into my belt.

Ragone was shouting, "Let's go, let's go. Let's fix those sons of bitches."

I started the car. "Now let me tell you something. You're not going to fix anybody. Just calm down. You're not going back in there thinking that maybe you're going to start shooting people down as soon as you see them. We go in there, and we take control without anybody getting killed. Now, if you haven't got the balls to do it that way, then get the hell out of the car right now. You understand me, Ragone?"

Ragone gave me an incredulous look, followed by one of anger at the unexpected reprimand. "Okay, I was just talking," he said in a subdued tone.

We drove back slowly without lights and parked two doors from the alley with the doors unlocked. We threaded our way through the alley. My mind went back to the guys in the apartment. Billy, the one who'd been at the door, was too big to take chances with, and I sensed that he knew what he was doing. Ralph, the one with the goatee, was nervous. A nervous man could be unpredictable, and that wasn't good. His partner had a gun, and I'd seen Mae grab a kitchen knife. She had to be a little crazy to be a whore in the first place, so since when do you expect rational behavior when it comes to whores? She'd slice me without a second thought if it was necessary.

If I were a John they'd never see me again. When you are a cop, you return. The idea was to con my way in and take over without anyone getting hurt. It's the way I operate. I haven't fired my gun in 17 years with the department. I've avoided it by using my head instead of the gun. Luck, and a few breaks from the man upstairs has also helped. If we kicked in the door to the apartment we'd be met with a barrage of bullets. Calling in backup men could bring the same results. I've seen it happen that way. It called for discretion. I told Ragone what I wanted. "We get in without guns showing, we have to get close, and when we've got the drop, we draw guns and make the arrest."

I knocked on the door, lightly. It opened a crack, and Billy's face peered out. "We're back," I said in a whisper, and the door opened all the way. In the dim light we could make the four of them out. Fred and Ralph held guns. Mae was still walking around bare-breasted.

I went in, trying to move casually, with Ragone one step behind me. I shook my head. "Man, you guys are something with those guns. What the hell you think we're trying to do? A little action is all we want, man."

Billy grinned, confident that he had it all under control and slipped his gun into his pocket. The man with the goatee still held the gun on us. Billy was my choice. He appeared to be the leader. It was logical to make him my ally. "What the hell is the matter with your friend?" I said to him and looked at the goateed man. "What the hell does he think he is, a cop or something?"

"Put that piece away, Ralph," Billy said. "You scaring the shit out of these boys." He grinned at me. "This boy couldn't get it up before and now you making it worse for him."

Ralph stuck his gun in his belt. He was standing on one side of the room along with the other man and Mae. Billy was behind me. I could imagine their plan. They'd try to learn if I had the money, and then I'd go into one of the bedrooms with Mae while Ragone waited his turn. They'd make their move while we were separated and they'd use knives to keep it quiet.

I wanted to get closer. I glanced at Mae and stepped over to her. I was close now. I looked into her eyes and saw the calculating coldness. She and the rest of them were all going to participate in the murders.

I glanced back. Ragone and Billy were standing side by side. I hoped that Ragone was ready. When you make your move, you'd better be convincing. It's a matter of psyching yourself up. You've got to know that you'll fire if you have to fire, and the guy looking into your gun has to believe that you'll do it. In a situation like that a cop has to come on strong.

I said, "Let's go, Mae. Let's make it." I opened the button on my jacket and drew the .38 and pointed it at Ralph and the goateed man. "Police. Freeze or you're all dead! I'll blow your heads off!"

Ragone covered Billy. "Not a move, you bastard," Ragone shouted. "Up, get your hands up high."

They cut the profanity out on television. But you're not at a tea social, and you've got little time in which to communicate. I reached down and lifted Ralph's gun from his belt. Then I handcuffed him to the junkie. Ragone had Billy facing the wall. He took his gun and slipped the cuffs on.

Mae made a break for the window. She ran as though she were going to dive right through it. I spun, grabbed her. She wriggled free. She was deceptively strong. I caught her again, slowed her down. Her fingernails raked my face, and she broke loose.

Ragone bounded across the room as she opened the window. He pulled her away and punched her jaw. She dropped as though she had been poleaxed. He was a big guy. He could have wrestled her down to the floor and subdued her. I said, "You didn't have to do that."

He flushed with anger. "Look at your face. What the hell are you talking about?"

The four people who'd been in bed were gone.

I motioned Ragone to the door. "Go call it in." He left wordlessly and returned after a few minutes. Soon there were the sounds of footsteps in the hall, and five cops showed up. I recognized John Beckerman, Richie Powers, Mike Perelli and Nick Nicosia.

Richie went through the apartment and came back quickly. "That kid who's in there on the bed, I can't wake her up. She looks like she's had an overdose. I'm going to call for an ambulance." His face was gray. "Christ. Did you see the kerosene cans and the roaches?"

Perelli came out. His face was pale. "The girl doesn't look as though she's going to make it," he whispered. He pointed at Ralph. "I arrested that son of a bitch twice last year. They should have thrown the key away on him. And look at the rest of this shit. Dear Christ, she's dead, as good as dead. She's a baby. She's just a kid."

I took Ragone's flashlight, went in and looked at the victim. She couldn't have been more than thirteen or fourteen. Her veins were collapsed. The needle scabs on her thin arms had ulcerated and left dried blood. I stared at her and thought of my own daughter in her own room with its small-flowered wallpaper. Music lessons and suburban crabgrass, church functions and her bright, shining face contrasting to a child who lay dying on a bed that reeked of kerosene. I recall whispering, "Dear God!"

Her hands were like ice. "Who called for the ambulance?" I cried, and Perelli hurried in.

"Ten minutes ago, Dave. Richie called it in."

"It's Friday night," I said. "They could be so busy they'll never get here." I threw my jacket over her body and picked her up and began walking out with her. Her head and arms bounced like a rag doll.

In the living room, Beckerman said, "Dave, maybe you ought to wait for the ambulance."

"Shut up! Get some light in the alley so I don't fall down carrying her. Move!"

Beckerman waited outside next to my car. "Put her in my car," he said gently. "I'll take her, Dave."

I put her in my car on the back seat. Beckerman said, "Dave, she's dead. Don't go killing yourself getting her to the hospital."

"Shut up, you!" I started it up and went out of there with the high beams on and the siren blasting, heading for Martland Hospital with Nicosia next to me.

Cars scattered out of my way. I tore down a one-way street and saw the startled face on an oncoming driver cursing me. Crossing Springfield Avenue, I almost hit a truck broadside. Nicosia shouted, "Watch it!" as I cut the wheel sharply to the left and missed the tailboard by an inch. The car careened across the avenue. We cut in and out of traffic and skidded to a stop at the hospital's emergency entrance. I charged in, carrying her in my arms, through the swinging door. A young nurse, startled at the sight, said, "Here," pointing at a table where she could be set down. An intern was summoned. He was young, bearded and fatigued.

"I think she's had an overdose," I said. "You've got to get all that junk out of her system."

He studied the girl then looked at me. "Please step outside."

Nicosia tugged at my arm. "Come on, Dave."

We waited on a bench in the corridor. Across from us a middle-aged couple wept softly. The emergency room of hospitals in the middle of the night are the places of nightmares. One of their children had been mangled in an automobile accident. What could anybody say to them?

We sat in silence for a while, and then Nicosia said, "Dave, she's dead." The young intern came out after ten minutes. He stared at me, saying nothing, and I knew she was gone.

Nicosia stood up and held his hand out to me. "Come on, Dave. Let's go home. I'll make the report out on her later."

"Can you call someone to get you?" I said.

"No problem," Nicosia said. "Are you all right, Dave?" he asked in a concerned tone.

"Yes," I said and went out and parked in the darkness.

I was forty years old and felt as though I were a hundred. I bent my head over the wheel and felt tears behind my eyes for the young girl who had died and the obscene waste of her life.

Sorrow can dig up the past. I wept remembering what had happened on a Sunday morning in my own household. I was a uniformed policeman then. I had one of those rare experiences when all the squalor, cruelty, waste, anguish and hopelessness one sees in life were all swept aside. I caught an emergency squeal that a three-year-old child was choking to death on a piece of charcoal that he had swallowed.

When I got there, I found a small black boy who to all outward appearances was dead. I remember his mother sitting like stone. She was past hysteria. I knelt and gave him mouth-to-mouth resuscitation. When that failed, I applied pressure to his ribs. I knew he was gone. I felt as though I had lost my mind. I blew into his mouth again. When I least expected it, I felt the smallest breath from his mouth. I couldn't detect a heartbeat, but the boy was alive. An ambulance arrived. I followed it to Newark Hospital and saw him rushed to the pediatric ward and placed in an oxygen tent. I watched him grow stronger, his little lungs expanding with each breath and each moment that passed. It was my triumph. The memory is crystal clear. I can see that little boy as he opened his eyes. He was frightened, and he began to bawl. Watching him, half-laughing, half-crying, I said, "Go ahead, son. Come on, I want to hear it. Come on, son, that's better." He was really bellowing then. I watched him come back to life. I saw him smile.

I was rich. I had the world's happiness in my hands. I was drunk with it. It was the finest moment in my life. Talk to a cop who has saved a life and he's ten feet tall. Bursting with it, I went home and told my family what had happened. My wife's glowing face mirrored my exultation. She was radiant.

I went back to my car. The rest of the tour was going to be a breeze. When I departed, my thoughts were that I could handle almost anything. I wasn't prepared for what came next. The dispatcher's voice cut in sharply. "David, get over to your house. Your wife called. There's something wrong with your son."

When it's your own, you have premonitions of disaster. I hit the turret flasher button and the siren and drove like a maniac. My wife's face was grim. "He's having trouble breathing," she said. She hadn't been able to reach our family doctor. Neighbors were called, and one of them reached her family doctor. My son kept saying that he couldn't get any air. When the doctor arrived, he gave him a shot, and when that didn't help, he tersely advised that we call an ambulance. "It's the epiglottis and his tonsils. They're badly swollen. Call for an ambulance."

The ambulance that arrived for my son was the same one that had carried the little black child to the hospital earlier in the day. The driver remembered me. He rushed my son to Newark City Hospital.

The doctors were the same doctors who had labored to save the little black child less than an hour ago.

They placed an oxygen mask over my son's mouth. It didn't help. Then they made an incision in his throat. When that failed, my five-year-old son died. He didn't make it.

In a forty-five-minute period I had saved a three-year-old child from choking to death and I had lost my own son in an identical situation.

I didn't know what to do. People who have known that type of tragedy can understand what it was like. The experience of saving a life and losing my own son within an hour was traumatic. The pain was like a fist squeezing my heart.

I didn't know that pain could be that hard. He was my firstborn son, a beautiful child. I didn't know what to do. I wanted to offer strength to my wife, and I couldn't find it. Her stricken face tore me apart.

I wanted to commit suicide, and there was the ever-present gun on my hip to do it with. Wiser heads among the police took the gun from me. I didn't know where I was.

I went home and wept and shouted, "God, why me? Why must it be me? Why did it happen this way? What had the boy done to deserve to die?"

Depression and mental problems came from his death. I couldn't live with it. Life became intolerable. I couldn't sleep. There were times when my anguish became so heavy that I would burst into tears. I began taking tranquilizers to help me function, and I became heavily addicted to drugs. I used them to help me forget what happened. After three or four hours the effect of the drug would wear off, and then when it no longer helped, I took more pills, three and four and even five. At the time I knew very little about drugs. They weren't a national problem seventeen years ago. I knew that I had four nephews who used them. Since drugs hadn't had any bearing on my own life, they were somehow looked upon remotely. My addiction was what really made me aware of the drug scene. I was running away, but there wasn't any place to run because four hours after I'd taken a pill I bounced right back to the pain of my son's death.

I don't ever remember coming down during that time and being rational. It's possible that I would have been addicted for a far longer period of time if it hadn't been for one of my drug-addicted nephews. He stopped me one day while I was stoned and he said, "You're as bad as I am. What's the difference between you and me?"

I looked at him and saw the needle marks on his arms and the collapsed veins. He'd been arrested many times for stealing and mugging for the money to support his habit.

Realization can come like getting a kick in the stomach. I knew he was right. I was addicted. If I continued, I had to lose my family. Stelazine, Valium and all the other tranquilizers just weren't doing the job for me anymore. Eventually I knew that I would go on to still stronger drugs.

I had a problem, and an addict had made me come face to face with it.

When I looked at him, I knew I had to stop. I realized how easy it was for anyone to get hooked on drugs. The direction of my life had to be changed. I knew I could no longer use drugs as my crutch. I began to see for the first time, after I became involved myself, what was happening in society, with my nephews and with young people. They were all running away from problems they couldn't face. Problems. Everybody has them. I used drugs to forestall unpleasantness and depression before they got to me. When you can't beat a problem without them, you're hooked.

It's hard to realize it in yourself. But I've been there, and the symptoms begin to appear when you can't wait to get home for the pill that you've been thinking about all day.

I went through it and I beat it. Nothing is easy. I've made up my mind to control my feelings and my thoughts so that when I have a problem, I don't take it out on my wife and my kids, no matter how bad it becomes. I go home to a hot bath. I talk to myself if it helps. I relax. I listen to music, work out. I work to the point of complete exhaustion. Work can take the place of addiction. And I found that I could beat it. The craving for the drugs passed. I can remember the way it was for me, counting the times I defeated it. And I grew stronger mentally each time it happened because that's where it's at, in the mind. With heroin and all hard drugs, it becomes physical as well, and it's tougher to beat.

I'm not attempting to pass myself off as an expert, nor am I offering an easy solution to a drug-oriented society. There isn't any. I'm not a superman, but I know what I've lived through. I know that if I can beat it, so can the next man or woman who falls victim to drugs.

CHAPTER TWO

The next day when I went in I asked Lieutenant Kendricks to assign Ragone to someone else. I knew that it was going to turn into an argument.

"I gave the kid to you so that he'd be out with an experienced hand," Kendricks said.

"That's what I figured, but I can't work with him."

Kendricks stared at me. "Come on into my office, Toma. I want to talk to you."

He sat at his desk, lit a cigar and said, "Shut the door, Dave." He was a lean, square-shouldered, blue-eyed, gray-haired man about fifty-five. As a foot patrolman he'd instilled fear and anger in the Central Ward with the use of his nightstick. There were complaints and department reprimands, which he ignored. Eventually he'd been given a desk job, and it was where he remained. He had been with the department for twenty-three years and had gained the reputation as a tough sergeant and even tougher lieutenant. A superior can be cold and demanding and often with good results as long as he is as demanding of himself as he is of his subordinates. But occasionally the lieutenant has to put himself in the same line of fire as his men. Kendricks played it safe and deceived no one on the squad.

"All right, Toma. We'll hear you first, about Ragone."

I told him about the prostitution detail that Ragone and I had worked. I went through it step by step and explained what had happened.

Kendricks nodded. "Now let me get this straight. You're telling me that he didn't follow your instructions and that he didn't wait in the car for you to return. Instead, he left the car and the guns, and then he managed to find the apartment by himself."

"Right. He left the car, followed me, saw me turn into the alley, and then he went back to the car and waited for me to return. When I didn't, he came back for me unarmed. He was supposed to wait until I went back and got him."

"From what I understand of the arrest, if he had a gun, then maybe you'd both be dead. You said that there were people in the apartment who had guns pointed at you when you first heard him calling your name out in the hall."

It was a good point. "That's right. I'm not saying that he didn't use good judgment." I paused. It was difficult. I didn't want to put the rookie down.

"Then what?" Kendricks said.

"It's just that I don't think that he should have come back after me without his gun. I think he's a little new at this to be trying it that way."

"You could have been hurt if he came in carrying a weapon," Kendricks said.

"The point I'm trying to make is that I had almost conned my way out of there when he showed up. I had to go through the whole con again when he came in. He had no way of knowing what I had said to talk my way out of there. Suddenly he was standing in the hall. We could both have gotten hurt if somebody lost his head. I didn't like him leaving unguarded guns in the car."

"I don't like to do this. I don't like to break up teams every time a guy isn't happy with his partner." He paused. "It's the last time I'm going to do it for you." He grinned without mirth. "You've got Jack Nichols."

"I'm not asking you for a different partner. Why give me anybody? I don't work well with other cops because they don't work my way. I get the work done right when I'm by myself."

"No, forget it. You've got Nichols."

I shrugged. It was over. Ragone was inexperienced, and Nichols had a vendetta against every addict in Newark. I would have preferred Ragone.

He tapped his fingertips together and said matter-of-factly, "Toma, I'm getting a little static about you, and I was asked to have a little talk with you. There are two things I want to discuss. We'll take them one at a time. First, I want to know what you think of the department?"

"I've heard of better and of worse."

"Ah, so you think this is worse?"

"I don't know of any police department that couldn't stand some improvement."

Kendricks closed his eyes for a moment, folded his arms, nodded, opened his eyes again. "No doubt you think that you're the man who thinks he can improve the department."

"I didn't say that. You asked me a question, and I told you what I thought."

That didn't satisfy him either. He said, "Do you know how

many men in this precinct are taking courses at the Police Academy and at colleges?"

I said, "About eight, I think."

"They're trying to make better law officers out of themselves. You agree with that?"

"Of course."

"You bet your ass, of course. That means this place will have a little dignity. Any objections to that?"

"None."

He tapped the folder on his desk. "We're trying to run this place the way it should be run, with some dignity, and you turn around and make it look like a circus."

I could feel anger rising. "How?"

"The press writes you up like you're some kind of hero. They think those disguises make interesting copy." He opened the folder and removed a copy of the *Star-Ledger*. "Look here. You're a telephone lineman, a hobo, doctor, priest. You're everything. Next thing you'll be the kitchen sink." He paused. "You've never had official permission to use them."

"Okay, but I get results using them."

"I've watched you since you became a cop. You discredit the department. You make it a laughing matter. You're an embarrassment. What the hell is a person to think when he picks up a newspaper and he reads about a cop they call the Actor and the man of a thousand faces? You're using the department as your own personal stage. I'm running a police department and not a theater."

"I operate the way I do because I get results with it. I've got thousands of arrests and a ninety-eight percent conviction record that goes with it. The disguises work. I can infiltrate with them. They allow me to get in real close so I can see and know what's going on in a hood's mind. That's one reason. There's another one. Gambling joints mysteriously moved when they were going to be raided."

"Are you trying to tell me that somebody tipped them off, some cop? Who is he?"

"Who knows? I know that when I go out on my own in disguise, when I can infiltrate and get the whole lowdown, who's involved, what's happening and where, I come up with quality arrests that stick. I've been getting the job done."

He glared at me. "You're a maverick. You don't want to walk like the rest of us. I've seen guys like you bounced off the force. They wind up as nothing."

"I'm still here," I said.

"You're grandstanding, is what the hell you're doing. Never mind what the hell you say you're trying to do with all those goddamn disguises. You're not fooling me with all that crap. I don't want you giving any more press interviews. You're an embarrassment to the department and that isn't the worst of it. Where do you come off disclosing your disguises? When you do that, you're divulging methods used in apprehending criminals. What the hell are you trying to do, tip them off on what they have to watch out for? How do you justify that? You want to give that a try? That's something you haven't explained to the press."

I said, "You maintain the disguises and you exert pressure on the guy on the street who's up to something. He reads about an undercover operator, about guys infiltrating narcotics and gambling and organized crime, and it throws him off stride. You create uncertainty in his mind. So he looks around, and he knows there is somebody out there who blends right into his own group, and he knows the guy who's out there stalking him doesn't look like a cop. It has to put pressure on him."

"So what? Now you tell me how this is going to help bust him."

"All right, he knows that there is a good chance an undercover cop is standing right next to him. So maybe he doesn't know where to look first and he doesn't know from which direction trouble can come at him. You put enough pressure on him, and he's going to blow it by overreacting. He's going to be looking over his shoulder more than he should, or else he's always looking around watching people, or he's furtive-looking and nervous. If he thinks there's an undercover cop lurking around it can be a deterrent to what he has in mind."

"Smart. You think you've got all the answers, Toma. What about the guy who appears happy and calm, as though he hasn't got a care in the world?" he said.

"A good cop can spot that kind of cover too. Maybe the guy is too calm, he's too much at ease, and maybe his little act is for the benefit of anybody he feels is watching him. The airports and the gambling casinos hire people with a trained eye to spot guys who look wrong. Customs inspectors have been doing it for years."

He stared at me with heavy skepticism. "Either way you're right."

I was getting tired of his questioning. He was too set in his ways to change his concepts about how a cop should operate. All he wanted was to play it safe. He'd view anyone who made waves with an unorthodox approach as somehow jeopardizing his own position. I started to get up. "Is there anything else, Lieutenant?"

"Where do you think you're going, Toma? I didn't say we were through here." A grin spread over his face. "The guy with all the answers. You've got a problem, Toma. You know Al Winters' Poolroom, over on Clinton?"

"I know it," I said, and already knew what he was about to say.

"You've been seen walking in and out of that joint for the last two weeks. That poolroom fronts for one of the biggest loan sharking rings in the state. It's a known hangout for hoods. What were you doing there?"

"I know what's going on. It's why I was there. I didn't spend my time shooting pool. I was trying to get a line on the place."

"You were seen talking to Mike Grabowsky. Every time you've been there you've been seen in this guy's company. So what the hell are you doing associating with Grabowsky? He was inside for seven years. Armed robbery is what we know about him. So he became your friend. Do you think we're stupid? What business do you have with him?"

The questioning was unwarranted. If a detective didn't have the leeway to associate with and to form contacts with criminals, then he couldn't function as a detective. I knew it, and so did Kendricks. It applies only when the department suspects that a cop is on the take. It didn't apply to me. Kendricks was using it as a method to apply leverage for his beef about the disguises and their publicity.

"What have you got on him now?" I said.

"Nothing. But we know his background, and he isn't clean. And you still haven't told me what you're doing associating with him."

"I can explain that. I knew him years ago, before he was sent up. He was peddling broads and setting guys up with broads and pictures. I knew him. He remembers me. So when I learned that he was hanging around Al Winters' place, I began to use him to help me walk in. I make friends of the opposition, and that's my game. A junkie can lead me to a pusher, and if I'm lucky, he can take me to a wholesaler or an importer. When I see Grabowsky, we talk about everything except what we're both doing there. We talk about broads and the Giants and about everything as long as it's got nothing to do with what's going on in the poolroom. Meanwhile, guys see me talking to Grabowsky, and they figure that I'm his friend, and they go about their business. So it gives me a chance to look around and maybe pick up a little useful information.

"Grabowsky knows that you're a cop. He did seven hard years on a twelve-year rap. Why the hell should he consider you or any cop his friend?"

"We grew up together. I knew him. When he was sent away, he wrote to me. His kid brother was getting into all kinds of trouble. He was clouting cars, and he was afraid the kid was going to take a fall. He wanted me to talk to him. The kid was eighteen then."

"Yeah, that makes a lot of sense. He's sitting inside because a cop sent him up, so he gets in touch with a cop to help straighten his kid brother out. What did you do, have a little man-to-man talk with the kid?"

"Something like that. When I saw it wasn't working, I took him down to the jail and showed him some of the sights. The kid was stealing cars and taking fast rides. So I took him to the morgue and showed him a kid who'd gone through the windshield and had his head cut off his shoulders. I explained that it could happen to him. It doesn't always work, but it worked for the kid. Maybe it straightened him out, or it had something to do with it. That was seven years ago. He's teaching high school chemistry now. I like to think I had something to do with that."

Kendricks looked past me. After a time he said very quietly, "I wouldn't be surprised. You know years ago I probably would have handled it the same way. I was the old-school cop, with a lot of street intelligence and common sense." He stared off into the past. "You knew people and their children by their first names. If I caught a kid stealing vegetables off a stand, I'd give him a boot in the ass and maybe I'd call his old man, or if I caught a kid doing something wrong, I'd bring him in and throw him in a cell. I wouldn't even book him. In most cases his parents wouldn't object. I'd just let him see what the hell jail was all about. I'd scare the ass off him. Do something like that today, and the parents would be down, threatening to sue you."

I said, "I know what you mean."

"Toma, I'm going to retire when I finish with this command. Anything that happens here is a direct reflection on me. I've been a cop for a long time, and I know what the hell is going on."

"I've had a bad evening and a bad morning," I said. "Lieutenant, why don't you get to the point?"

Kendricks measured his words carefully. "You're making heavy gambling arrests, and you're going about it by using those crazy disguises. That gets a lot of publicity. Sooner or later somebody is going to start shoving heavy bread under your nose to get you to lay off the drops and the banks." He slammed his fist on the desk top. "If that hasn't already happened." His eyes went small. "I don't want to retire any sooner than I have to. The innocent get hurt, as well as the guilty, when that happens, and I don't want to retire any sooner than I have to. Do you understand, Toma?"

I said, "Sure," and walked back to my desk. I went out, got into my car, drove off and parked down at the port area. I understood Kendricks' concern. It was a matter of survival for him. He didn't want anybody jeopardizing his future. I couldn't blame him for that. It wasn't the first time that I'd listened to the same reprimands and accusations and threats, but I knew I was right. A cop doesn't spend his time in a Rectory when he wants information. He associates with sleazy cruds and informants and guys awaiting trial who are trying to make deals for reduced sentences.

It's a known fact that a detective's success depends almost entirely on the sources of information at his disposal and his willingness to put in the extra effort and time to check out the tips he has received. He has to follow them up. It takes legwork and sacrifice and spending time away from home. He pays a heavy price in mental and physical health. He reasons that he can't take it all to heart and bring it home with him if he is to last his tour of duty with the department. He never forgets the way it was when he was a patrolman. As a cop he pounds a beat in sub-zero weather and freezes his tail, and if he ducks into a warm spot to grab a smoke, there's always the possibility that a gumshoe will spot him and make a complaint. He puts up with cop haters and the snipers. The public stands ready to accuse the entire police force of corruption because they've heard of a cop shaking down a hooker or making a deal with a bookmaker.

The conversation with Kendricks had left me feeling disgusted. He wanted me to change my methods. I had made many quality gambling arrests. Important top crime people had been jailed and organized crime had threatened my family as a result.

So why not ease off? What are you trying to prove, Toma? You don't have to be a genius to know that every time you con your way into a place and con your way out you increase the odds of getting hurt. What kind of glory do you think you'll find in some whore's grimy pad? Or is it glory you're really looking for? Maybe I'm playing the game on time that's already run out. It could be. And maybe you hate the sight of the ghetto because you know that unless you change your methods, it's where you could die.

Nobody could accuse me of anything if I eased off. Life could be simpler and a lot easier. I could increase the odds that I'd last a little longer. So who could fault me for that? Not my wife and four children. You want to work alone. You want to be your own man. Who wouldn't like to be able to live his life without worry about rules made by someone else? It was unfair to Pat and the kids. They'd miss my presence if I was out of their lives. I'd seen too many fatherless homes.

I thought of my problem with Kendricks and called Police Director Domenick "Dick" Spina. I was sure that he had other things to concern himself with other than a detective who felt that he was getting a hard time from a superior. But when you've got a problem, you talk to friends, and Spina was a friend.

A girl answered and said, "Hold on, please, Director Spina is on another line."

I waited and thought of Domenick Spina. Newark has more police proportionately to its population than any city in the country. Spina was probably one of the best police directors and administrators that city ever had. If he had a flaw, it was his impatience with subordinates who wouldn't do what they were supposed to do. Spina was a man who wanted action and results from his men. He was a man who never stopped trying to make things better for Newark's underprivileged. He had instituted programs to help them. I owed Spina. He had promoted me to detective.

One of the reasons for my appointment to the bureau had come about as the result of a squeal I'd taken while I was a radio car patrolman in 1961. My partner was Joe Murray. A 300-pound woman had gone berserk (we learned later that she was a recently released mental patient) and was throwing dishes and furniture from the window of a third-story apartment on South Orange Avenue. As we knocked on her door, it opened unexpectedly, and a thrown chair hit Murray and dropped him to the floor. The apartment was a scene of complete chaos. She ran back and forth, screaming hysterically. She threw whatever she could get her hands on. Murray went to the car to call for additional help.

I had my hands full trying to quiet her. I decided to leave her alone until help arrived. When she ran toward a window with what appeared to be an attempt to jump, I threw my arms around her. An attempt to bring her down to the floor proved to be difficult. She had great strength, and her actions were unpredictable.

Rolling about on the floor, she bit my hand and my neck. Overpowering a man can be easier. There are ways that can be employed to stop resistance. They can be painful. It's different with a woman. She got to her feet. I kept yelling, "I'm trying to help you." She ran at me, clawing my face with her fingernails, screaming insanely. I didn't want to hurt her, and yet I knew that if she could kill me, she would. The idea was to subdue her without physical injury. It didn't work. We wrestled our way out into the hall, to the top of the stairs. She kicked me in the chest, and I fell backward, tumbling end over end down twenty-two stairs. Spina, charging up the stairs, saw it all happening. Soon additional police arrived, and an ambulance. An attempt to get to my feet brought agonizing pain. I was carried off in a squad car to the hospital. The woman was placed in a restraining jacket and driven off to Martland in an ambulance.

The diagnosis was a herniated disc in my spine, and I was hospitalized in traction for six weeks. It was a low point in my life. My legs were completely paralyzed. I feared I wouldn't walk again. Spina visited me and told me that he liked the restraint I had used handling the mental patient. I remember saying, "I'm not sure that I'd handle it the same way if I had it to do over again."

"Sure you would," said Spina.

I can remember turning my head so Spina couldn't see the tears that coursed down my face and sobbing, "I can't move my legs."

"You can do anything you want to do, Toma," he said in an unnaturally gruff voice and left the room.

I remained in the hospital for six weeks while sensation slowly returned to my legs. I was discharged and went home to recuperate. Altogether I was out for four months. For a brief period of time I had known the agony of the handicapped. I could never again dismiss them from my mind or accept their lives matter-of-factly.

When I reported back for duty, I was informed that Spina wanted to see me.

He smiled and said, "What did I tell you? You look better than ever, Toma."

I said, "Thank you."

Spina said, "Toma, I'm appointing you detective. I've checked your record. You've done a good job in the patrol cars. You're conscientious and energetic, and you put in more hours than you have to. You don't look like a detective, and that could make you more effective."

He understood even then.

"Toma, the man who appoints you puts his neck out. If you don't work out, it comes right back at him. I want you to do the job right."

I thanked him.

Spina offered me his hand and said, "Good luck, Dave Toma."

I went out elated. There are very few cops who don't have the hope of making the Detective Bureau, and I was no different. I'd thought of it many times as a foot patrolman and then as a radio car officer. I'd been struck by the sharp division and lack of communication between the uniformed cop and the detective squad. I'd always hoped that one day I'd make the detective squad and always believed that it would happen. When it did, I already knew that the key to becoming a good detective lay in good relationships between the detective and the man on the beat. He was the detective's eyes and ears. Realizing his true worth and communicating with him was the key. It has never changed for me.

Detectives tend to regard themselves as an aloof segment of the department, separate and apart from the man in uniform. It's a mistake. He dresses differently, and he has a special glamor and status. Nevertheless, there isn't a detective who doesn't realize that the uniformed cop is always visible. The mentally deranged and the contemptible sniper kill uniformed cops. He's there, and he's a target.

Spina got on the phone. "Hello, Dave. Are you the real Dave Toma, the man the newspapers call the man of a thousand faces?" He laughed. "Glad to hear from you."

"That's me," I said.

"What's happening?" he asked.

Spina is a busy man, so I got right to the point and told him about Kendricks.

"Is there anything to what he says?" Spina said.

I explained my thoughts for putting pressure on the criminals, and Spina listened and interrupted from time to time with an, "Oh, yes."

When I finished, he said, "I understand how Kendricks feels but I agree with your thoughts and methods. We're better off preventing crime."

"You want me to tell him that?"

"No, I'll talk to him. Don't worry about it. Just do your job." He paused. "How are the wife and kids?"

"Fine, just fine, thank you."

"How's your back?"

I said, "Eh!"

"Come on, what are you complaining about?" said Spina.

I said, "Thank you, sir. Good-bye," and I hung up.

One thing was certain. Domenick Spina is an honorable man and Spina backed me only because he felt I was right and for no other reason. That's the way it is with Spina. I recall a Presidential commission reporting his complete fairness during the Newark riots.

CHAPTER THREE

My family and I live in a modest home in the suburbs. For years we'd lived in Newark's central city. We'd been a part of the slums. You never forget your background. It can be something like the little patch of green grass in your backyard that needs cutting that brings your mind back to the slums where there is no grass.

Newark is a divided city, for business-commerce, and the adjoining slums. The city is cramped by its small land area of 23.6 square miles, one-third of which is Newark Airport and unsuitable salt marshland. The city has nowhere to expand. During the daylight hours the population more than doubles with suburbanites who work there. They contribute nothing to property taxes. Per capita cost for municipal services, police and fire protection have reached ridiculously high figures. The tax rate for its residents has assumed outrageous proportions.

No public service is delivered without money, and since Newark's money comes essentially from property taxes, it's a foregone conclusion that it can't raise enough money to meet its needs. The upshot is that Newark's educational system has made its youngsters expendable. The dropout rate is estimated at nearly 45 percent. Overcrowding, double sessions, absenteeism, inadequate materials and reading levels are consistently below the national level.

Newark is an abandoned stepchild. Its health and welfare costs are twenty times higher than surrounding areas. Health problems are almost beyond solution. It leads the country in the number of babies who die in the first year, the young mothers who die in childbirth and the residents who contract tuberculosis.

The business center of Newark is about a mile and a half square and is crowded with banks, towering steel and glass office buildings, restaurants and department stores. From a distance the city appears affluent. But at the very edge of the business district and completely surrounding it are the slums, replete with crime, disease, corruption and heavy narcotics addiction. There are hundreds of acres of homes that have been leveled, and the land has become a dumping ground for trash. Conditions for the residents of the area, as well as the police, are always hazardous, but at night the muggers make safety conditions even more intolerable. A well-dressed man walking the streets alone is almost certain to get ripped off. In the criminal jargon, getting "yoked with a shank," which means attacking a stranger from behind by placing an arm around his neck, then putting a knife to his throat, is an every-night occurrence. At night the business area is deserted. Stores and restaurants close early. Thousands of junkies circulating through the city and the business area at night make Newark a no-man's-land with one of the highest crime areas in the country.

These aren't hopeful signs for any city. Still, I believe that a city like Newark which is a seaport and part of the Greater New York City area has to come back, and not because of a man's concern for his fellowman, but mainly for economic reasons. I'm optimistic enough to believe that but also to know that the money has to come in from outside the city.

Over the years Newark has had a lot of bad publicity. Former Mayor Hugh Adonizzio is serving a prison term for Mafia-linked corruption. It had a race riot in which twenty-nine persons were killed and block upon block of buildings were burned and destroyed. Organized crime on the east coast set up its headquarters in New York, New England and New Jersey. In New Jersey they settled in Newark.

My father, Vincent, is eighty-nine years old, and I am privileged that he is still alive. My mother, Jennie (Vincenza) as she was called, by her family and friends in Italian, died six months ago. They were married for sixty-five years, and he has taken her death badly. He lives alone in a wood frame house in Newark's central ward ghetto, and I see him daily. There are times when he stares off into space and his eyes fill with tears. He stands straight, he is coherent and alert, senility has spared him so far. Observing him, I feel some of his pain, and I look away. He is a proud man. What can I say to him?

My mother was a Pentacostal Evangelist in the First Church of Christ. I can recall her missionary work. As a child I can remember her getting stale bread from Taystee, Fisher and Bond and giving it to the poor. She had twelve children, and three died. Infant mortality is higher for the impoverished. I am the youngest. Her mission took her into Newark's worst jails, where she preached the Word of God and attempted to change the direction of the inmate's lives. She always had a good word for felons and regarded them as children who had lost their way. Her pulpits were skid row, a street corner in the ironbound district, a home where children had been abandoned or one where there was sickness and poverty. She wasn't a sophisticated woman. She believed that if someone needed help, you did whatever you could for them. It's a good way to live.

We shuttled from house to house when my father could not find work and the rent couldn't be paid. For a short period of time we were on home relief, what is called welfare today. It was a low point in my father's life. When it occurred, he spoke to no one and didn't look at us. The children slept four in a bed. The apartments were roach- and rat-infested. I was bitten as a child. At night when a rat came into the darkened apartment, my father banged the walls with his fists while switching the lights on and off and tried to destroy the enemy as it scurried for safety.

My sisters tell me that I was a momma's boy. She attended church every evening of the week and took me with her. I was the baby. When she worked, I was left with my sister Tess, and I was occasionally shuttled back and forth between my other sisters. I was shy and introverted. When I was four, I developed a nervous tic, and even now at moments of stress it occurs.

Eventually my father found employment as a tailor in a New York sweatshop, where he labored for fourteen hours a day on shoulder pads. He was beset with financial hardships and the weight of providing a living for all of us. Disobedience on my part would be met with a threat: "You don't behave and do what you're told I'm going to give you to the cops."

As a result, I was afraid of police. My father loved me then, as he has always loved me, but the threat of punishment by the police was an accepted practice in those days. He had emigrated from Foggia, Italy, and like most immigrants, he held a distrust and fear of the police. Somewhere along the line I also developed a fear of fire engines. It seems that I had a three-year-old cousin who lived with my mother when she was a young girl in Brooklyn. He played with matches one afternoon and burned the house down to the ground. In the middle of the night the family fled to Newark. The event was spoken of in whispers for years.

I was a child in the Depression years while my father struggled to make a home in the world for himself and his family. He worked steadily and dreamed of having a house of his own. It became his goal. My mother pitched in and made artificial flowers at home in the late evening. The entire family helped, working into the early hours of the morning. It was piecework, and the rate was $1 a gross. On Saturday morning I helped my father deliver them to New York.

The dream materialized and came true. He bought a three-story wood frame house. We occupied the ground level, and there were two families above. My father became a different man. He walked with the pride of ownership. There was a small piece of land behind the house, and he grew tomatoes, cucumbers, peppers and summer squash, and as the plants grew, so did my father's happiness. But it was the Depression, and in those days not many people could afford rent in Newark's ghetto, let alone find food.

The tenants couldn't pay the rent, and my father couldn't find it in himself to evict them. The sheriff posted a foreclosure notice, and my father lost his house. It was a crushing blow for us all. Late one evening I heard him weeping in the kitchen and my mother's words, "Don't worry, Vincent. It will be all right. We have each other. God will take care."

I don't ever recall him saying that he loved any of us. He told me that he did by his toil and his sweat. I recall him coming home on a summer evening so tired and bent that he couldn't walk. He managed to provide a roof over our heads and enough food to feed us. How do you measure a man's worth? He would have died before he let harm come to us. He gave, my mother gave, they cared, and they loved us. They are good people, nothing more has to be said.

When I was fifteen, I was slight of stature. Newark was a rough place where the strong abused the weak. I came home bloodied time and time again, and my father said that I had to fight back.

I protested that I did, but that they were just stronger.

He stared at me for a while and said, "We'll make you stronger." Shortly thereafter he returned with a set of secondhand barbells and weights.

I conscientiously went to work, and six months later it paid off when my chief tormentor received more than he handed out when he tried pushing me around on the street. I became a physical culturist, and it changed my image of myself. I ran the high hurdles in school and learned to box. In later years there was a baseball scholarship offered from Duke University. I chose instead to play in the Phillies' farm system in the Canadian Provincial League for two years. As a marine I won the middleweight boxing championship at Parris Island. The weights had paid off.

I could not have accomplished what I've done in later life without the help, understanding and patience of my wife, Patricia. I doubt that any other woman would have put up with my eccentricities for as long as she has. I met her when I was

seventeen and she was fifteen. We were on a double date. I was
out with her girlfriend, and Pat was with another boy. When I
saw her, I immediately asked her out, and she was shocked that
I had asked while she was seeing my friend.

Later on leave from the Marines, I asked her out again. When
I saw her, I said, "You're the girl that I'm going to marry. You're
special."

She stared at me and said, "You're crazy."

We were married when I was discharged from the Marine
Corps. I took examinations for the State Police and the Newark
City Police. The results of the city tests came in first, and I went
to work walking a beat on a 7 P.M. to 3 A.M. shift for the first
three years. The next two years were spent in radio cars in the
Fourth Precinct. The car was number 43. The sector was one of
the busiest crime areas in the country. From the beginning I
didn't get along with Captain Heatherly. He disapproved of
befriending dope addicts. His method was to rule by fear.

As a result, I was constantly up before him. He delivered
lectures on the role of the policeman and how he was supposed
to instill fear and thereby gain respect. He disapproved of my
associating with addicts and criminals in an attempt to get
them back on the right track. His favorite expression was:
They'll eat you up and make a fool of you. The cop is the
military, and he rules, and he doesn't have to worry what the
people think.

Once he made the mistake of saying, "Toma, off the record
and man to man, what have you got to say? I want your opinion.
I want to know exactly how you feel about what I've been
telling you. Just say what's on your mind. No matter what you
say, it's okay."

"It's bullshit," I said. "The cop who gets along with people is a better cop because of it. I don't believe in mean, hard cops. They went out with the Johnstown flood."

His face purpled. He sprang from his chair and waved a fist at me. "Toma, you belong in a nuthouse under psychiatric care. You're crazy."

I protested. "You told me to speak man to man."

"I don't care what the hell I told you. You're nuts."

The Heatherlys are a vanishing breed. For every cop like Heatherly, I know thousands of policemen who are genuinely concerned with mankind. I believe that the average policeman is a warm, compassionate human being. He worries about his family, his personal safety, rent, mortgage and the tragedies that can befall us all. And with it he sees more than his share of the world's misery. He is affected by it. I've seen hardened, tough cops bawl, and I've seen them give of themselves. They're not perfect, but who is? They'll lend a hand to another human being in trouble.

To get back to Heatherly. My troubles with him, it seemed, had just begun. There were two incidents that triggered his punishment for me. The first took place on a cold October evening. Somebody had called in with a complaint that children had been crying in an apartment for eight hours. I took the call and found three black kids who had been abandoned. There were two boys of three and five and a girl of eight. They hadn't eaten in two days. I couldn't get myself to take those kids to the county shelter in the middle of the night. I loaded them into the car, drove around with them for half an hour until my tour of duty was over and took them home. I still lived in the ghetto then.

My wife answered the door. The three-year-old slept on my shoulder, and his brother and sister clung to my hands. She

I spoke their language. "What's wrong with you guys? What difference does it make what the guy's batting average was? I'll give you my phone number. Call me up. I'll find out exactly what the guy batted. Meanwhile, you boys use your heads. Everybody shake hands and walk off friends. That makes sense, and I can see you're all hip guys. The other way it becomes a big deal."

"How big a deal?" one of them asked.

"First of all, there's me and eight of you. That's hardly fair. What I would do to make it fair is for you to call all your brothers, that way you'll have about a hundred and twelve guys opposing me. That will make it even."

One of them grinned. "This man's all right."

"Give me five," I said, and shook hands with all of them.

Unknown to me, Parkinson had driven up in an unmarked car and had watched the entire incident. He couldn't have been more than twenty feet away. He walked over, grinning, as they were leaving. "I liked the way you handled that, Toma. What did you say to those kids? You broke them up."

"I kidded with them, a little jive talk."

He said, "They were your friends when they left."

I said, "That's the name of the game." It always was, and for a policeman who uses his head it always will be. You avoid the confrontation if you can. You make friends of the opposition. I've arrested people. I've kidded with them, I've kept it light, and I've always allowed them to retain their dignity. You don't curse anybody. You try to make him your friend. You don't put him down.

Name a good cop and a hundred names pop into your mind. I've already told you that I wasn't going to name those who were a pain in the ass.

I liked working with Sheriff Ralph D'Ambola. He was flamboyant, always kidding around. There was a jailbreak at the Newark jail, and when somebody set fire to the roof, the thought was that some prisoners were trapped up there. So I went up with him, and we were walking around the burning roof, and Ralph was making jokes. "Toma, if this roof gives way, there's going to be Roasted Sheriff and Detective on the menu for the boys inside the jail. Those guys are tough enough to eat us up."

One of the inmates was my nephew Ronnie, who'd been arrested for car theft. He took part in the break, and while attempting to jump from the wall, broke both his ankles.

Inspector Charley Zizza is a good cop and a personal friend. Twelve years ago when I had first started using disguises he had been my severest critic. Disguises were considered improper attire.

I walked in one morning wearing an engineer's helmet, a sweat shirt, work pants and muddy laborer's shoes. There were about fifteen detectives in the squad room immaculately dressed in sport jackets and business suits. That's the way it was in those days. It was as though they were advertising the fact that they were detectives.

Zizza called me into his office, looked me up and down and said, "What the hell is this? Where do you think you're going dressed like that?"

I explained that I was working on a gambling ring that was operating inside the Ballantine Brewery and that I was doing a little excavating outside one of the buildings as a method of infiltrating.

Zizza nodded. "That's nice. What are you doing, digging a tunnel so you can work your way in?"

"No, I'm digging a large hole in the road."

Zizza held up his hand like a traffic cop. "Hold it right there.

Crazy, that's all I need. This is the Police Department, not the Department of Public Works. Where's the authority to dig holes in the road?"

"I've got some friends in the road construction business. When I'm finished with the case I'll fill the hole and they'll retar it."

He stared past me. "A hole in the road, huh? How big are you making it?"

"I'm down about five feet."

"A five-foot hole," he said in a tone of wonderment. "Now tell me exactly what digging this hole has to do with busting a gambling ring at the Ballantine Brewery."

"Everything," I said.

"Everything. All right, tell me everything," Zizza demanded.

"Okay, it's like this. I'm digging this hole, and I've got a pick and two shovels and a bucket that I keep filling with water. They've got some goof-offs working in the brewery who use anything as an excuse to keep from working. So in the beginning I asked them where I could fill the pail with water, so a couple guys volunteered and brought me a filled pail."

"I see," Charles Zizza said. "And what did you tell them that you needed the water for?"

"That's a good question. First off, I've already told them that I was with the Department of Public Works and that I'm looking for a water main that was put in fifty years ago and that its location was lost. But there are blueprints that show the main is somewhere in the vicinity of the brewery."

"The water, the water. What do you tell them? Why do you need the water?"

"I need the water to wash away the earth, so I can see the

main if it's there and so I don't take any chances of breaking it with the pick. Anyway, these guys and I are getting real friendly, and now that they know me they allow me to go into the building to get my own water. I've got a lunch pail, and we stop and have lunch together."

He wrinkled his forehead. "Toma, you're in rare form today. I don't want to know any more about the excavation. In fact, you never told me about it."

I said, "Yes, sir."

I went back to the brewery the next day and placed a bet with the number writer. When the pickup man arrived later that afternoon to collect the numbers, I followed him to a poolroom which was the numbers drop. Armed with warrants, a squad busted the drop and the ring at the brewery two days later.

Charley Zizza called me in again and said, "Good job, Dave."

He did some good jobs himself. I can remember working a prostitution detail one evening and calling in for a few backup men. Zizza got on the phone, asked what the particulars were and then came down himself to act as my backup man. It isn't the usual line of work for an Inspector. Lookouts, prostitutes and pimps will use guns and knives to avoid arrest. I've run into some prostitutes who were every bit as rough as men.

When I saw Zizza at a designated corner, he explained his presence by saying that the precinct was so busy that all the men had been pulled out and he had come instead.

I can recall Zizza during the Newark riots of 1967. A good part of the department and the National Guard had become disorganized. Riots were a relatively new thing. Nobody had been trained to handle them. Thousands of rounds of ammunition were fired unnecessarily. It was Charley Zizza who organized a band of policemen and led them down Springfield

Avenue while it blazed and the din of gunfire was frightening. It was told to me later by his men that Zizza had said, "I've known these people for years. I don't want anybody killing anybody. Now let me get up front where they can see me." Charley Zizza. During the Newark riots, he stood ten feet tall.

CHAPTER FOUR

In the morning I was back at my desk to do my report on the arrest. I found a call slip with a phone number on it. There was no name. I dialed the number. A girl's voice answered, "Durkin, Gelfand and Planck, Investments."

I knew Andrew Durkin. "Mr. Durkin, please. Tell him it's David Toma."

"This is in reference to what please?"

"I'm returning his call."

She was a very efficient type. "I'm sorry, he's in conference. If you care to leave a message—"

"No message. Write my name down and hand it to him. That's all you have to do. He'll be very annoyed if you don't do it."

"Well, I don't know."

"Now, please," I coaxed. "Just do as I say."

"One moment, please," she said. The moment turned out to

be three minutes, and I had time to think about Andy Durkin. I'd run into him by accident over a year ago. I'd tailed some numbers guy to a motel on Route 56. He'd parked and gone into one of the rooms, and while I sat in my car on the parking lot, a door in one of the other units burst open suddenly, and a tall gentleman, completely nude and holding his trousers in one hand, took off running for dear life. There was another guy, fully clothed, right on his heels.

They thundered down the steps and tore across the parking lot and around the corner of the building. When I got there, I had a momentary glimpse of the nude man heading toward the Jersey swamps. The other guy was nowhere in sight. So I went after the guy holding the trousers. When I overtook him, I identified myself and asked what the hell was going on.

He put his pants on.

He was reluctant to tell me what was happening. In fact, he reminded me that he as a citizen had every right in the world to do as he pleased. If he wanted to run around naked, that was his business. Furthermore, he added all he wanted was to be left alone.

I was annoyed by the whole thing and became even more annoyed when I saw the car that I had been tailing scooting out of the parking lot. He was gone.

"Listen," I said. "I want your identification, and then I'm going to call your wife and ask her what the hell her husband is doing running around in the middle of the night, bare-assed."

That sobered him up real fast. He produced his driver's license. He gave me a sad story, one that I've heard many times. He'd stopped for a few drinks at the motel's bar and he had met a young lady who had given him a rub and a smile filled with promises of pleasure and goodies that awaited him in Room 19. She'd told him they would have to be quick and that he should get undressed as soon as he got there, since her husband would be back in an hour.

He had considered the bit with the girl an unexpected bonus. He assured me that it was the first time in his life that anything like this had ever happened to him. In the room he had disrobed quickly. There was a sound at the door, but instead of a dark-eyed beauty with fast hips, the man who barged in was massive and ugly with a broken nose and a threatening manner and he carried a blackjack.

"I take the cash and you just shut up and you don't get hurt," he announced. There was a small scuffle. The attacker was a bumbler. He swung the sap, missed, and it dropped from his hand. There was some running around, jumping over the bed and dodging. When the attacker tripped, Durkin grabbed his pants and fled through the door. And that was where I had come in.

"He didn't have a chance," Durkin said proudly. "Did you notice the way I outdistanced him? I ran the half mile at Yale. Set all kinds of records while I was there."

The night was a washout. I'd lost the numbers guy, and Durkin hadn't done anything that he could be charged with. Indecent exposure. Never. The man was running for his life. I'd seen it. He offered me a drink and a $20 bill. I turned them both down. He shook my hand and said, "I owe you a favor." And that was the last I'd seen or heard of Andrew Durkin.

He was on the phone. "Hello, Toma. How are you?" he said in a voice exuding warmth.

"Fine," I said.

When you're a city cop, information comes to you from unexpected sources. It can be a guy with a grudge or hatred of someone, someone who feels he's been wronged, an informer, both paid and unpaid, for self-gain in one way or another, and a guy who thinks he owes you a favor. Durkin got right to it. He spoke quietly.

"I owe you a favor for being discreet and tactful, and I like to square my accounts. I was in a barbershop over on Hawthorne. I had a dinner engagement last night, and there wasn't any time to go to my regular barber, so I stopped at this place on the way home. He was reluctant to take me. In fact, he was downright rude. While I was on the chair, he was interrupted about five times by people giving him slips of paper. I believe those were lottery numbers that he was taking. He hardly paid any attention to what he was doing, and the result was that he gave me a haircut that was absolutely laughable. It was so bad I had to cancel my business dinner."

Crazy? Like from out of left field. Durkin wanted to get even with the barber.

"Thank you," I said. "Is there anything else?"

"No, that's it. I feel that illegal lottery should be broken in this state, and I'm sure you feel the same way. I know you'll do something about it."

"Absolutely," I said, and hung up. Durkin didn't give a damn about illegal lottery. Durkin wanted the barber's hide because of the cruddy haircut.

I went to work, disguised as a street cleaner with a push broom, cart and handlebar mustache. It gave me all the time I needed for my preliminary surveillance. The barbershop was on the street level of a three-story red brick apartment building. As I looked at the storefront, the door to the apartment was at the left. There was a peephole in the door and no lock. Instead, there was a door handle with which to push the door open and a button which could be pressed. It figured that somebody inside would buzz back so that you could gain entry.

From what I could see, Durkin's account wasn't completely

correct. Numbers were being taken at the address, but it wasn't the barber who took them. He was cutting hair. There was a man sitting at a table in the back of the store who was running the operation. He was busy. During an hour's interval about fifteen players dropped in to give him the action, which he wrote on slips. He then went out into the street, buzzed at the door leading to the apartments above the shop and went up-stairs.

Getting into the hallway so that I could determine where he took the slips could be tricky. I doubted that the door could be forced without revealing giveaway signs or ruining the electric lock mechanism. By noon my street cleaner disguise had about as much exposure as it could take without blowing my cover.

Sam Bleeker is a friend. He is a wizened and weather-beaten old guy who owns a hot dog umbrella wagon on Bergen and Clinton. It was about four blocks away.

"Now let me get it straight," Bleeker said. "You want to borrow my cart for the afternoon and whatever you take in you hand over to me. Is that right?"

"That's it," I said.

"Where you gonna work?"

"Over on Hawthorne."

"Sounds good." Bleeker grinned and pointed at me. "You work and I'm going to take in a movie." We made arrangements for returning the cart to him. He supplied me with a fresh apron and the deal was made.

Pushing the cart back, I was hailed four times. "Hey, hot dog, hey, hot dog, give me a couple with onions." I did some business. I parked the cart in front of the barbershop and resumed my surveillance for three hours, and sold $35 worth of hot dogs. I observed that the writer was getting heavy action.

I could figure out what happened next. The lottery winning

number for the day was tabulated on the handle of certain races, on an out-of-state racetrack. The cutoff time for accepting bets had to be strictly observed. If anyone had advance information on what the first number was, the numbers bank would soon be bankrupt. It figured. At twenty minutes before post time the lottery writer left and made his way upstairs again. And in the time remaining to post time, the barber took the play and then carried it upstairs himself with a few minutes to spare. That explained what had annoyed Durkin while he was getting his haircut. The barber was merely filling in for the numbers writer.

Getting a collar on the lottery writer and even the barber would have been easy, but I wanted the numbers drop and the people who were operating it in the apartment.

I returned the hot dog cart to Bleeker, paid him and drove off. It was going to be tough getting into the upstairs apartment. Cases do not solve themselves, through either coincidence or carelessness. Guys who are violating the law know it. They are on guard, and they rarely make things easy for you. I believe that if you force movement by creating unexpected situations for the people you're trying to apprehend, then you have a better chance of something happening that will expose their methods of operation and that will allow you to get in close.

I drove back to the center of town, parked my tired '63 Valiant and went to the Board of Health. I was something of an oddity to the trim redhead with the green eyes who listened to my request. She'd never heard of one like it before. She stared at me.

"Oh, I don't think so, sir. I can't give you a Health complaint form."

I flashed my shield. "it's official police business."

She mulled it over and said, "One moment. I can't do that on my own. I'll have to get Mr. Revere's okay. He's my superior," she explained.

"Of course, thank you."

She hurried off, went into a glass cubicle, explained it and came back. "He's in there. You can go in." She looked relieved. She was off the hook.

Revere was in his sixties, gray-haired, apprehensive and suspicious. So you give them what they want to hear. Tell him that you want the form to gain entry illegally and he envisions repercussions. We shook hands, and I flashed the badge again. That always helps. "Mr. Revere, we have an ugly situation here, and it's being perpetrated through the use of Health complaint forms."

"My forms!"

"No. They're counterfeit. There's a man who has been going around to different restaurants writing complaints for dirty glasses and insanitary conditions. He's accepting bribes."

Relief flashed over his face. This was something that he would understand. "They'll stop at nothing today," he declared indignantly.

"Absolutely nothing. I'm checking around with the local printing shops. I'll need the form to determine if they've had requests to print them up. I didn't want to go into it with the girl at the desk." I gave him a man-to-man smile. "I'd like to keep it quiet."

"Of course." He left and came back with a manila envelope. I thanked him and searched the hall of records and learned that the building on Hawthorne was owned by Donald G. Harmon and that he resided there. I drove back to the precinct, checked out and went home.

There's an old saying that you don't know the lady until you

79

marry her, and even then you need a measure of luck. I'm one of the lucky ones. I finished supper, and I thought about the lottery drop. I was preoccupied. When it's like that, my wife has the wisdom to ignore me. It can give you the time to think of your next step. I had it straight in my mind when I went to sleep.

At nine in the morning the barber had no customers, but the lottery writer already had a brisk walk-in business going. Sitting in my parked car a block away, I counted ten people who entered the shop and left within a minute or two.

Trying the doorbell on the street door brought no results. I imagined the only way the door would be opened was when the correct signal was given on the street buzzer. Getting close enough to observe what the signal was would be very difficult, if not impossible, even with the use of binoculars.

I strode into the barbershop. In the official capacity of a Board of Health inspector one can throw fear into the hearts of those who have violated sanitary conditions. "I'm from the Board of Health," I announced. "Where can I find the landlord?"

An official in any capacity can make a con man or a thief or almost anybody nervous. The lottery writer and barber were no exceptions. I wore a mustache, a wig and a dark business suit with white shirt and conservative tie, and even before I had finished making my announcement, the lottery writer had already thrown his slips into a drawer in his table.

The barber was a short man, thinning on top with a worried look on his face. "What's wrong? We got no complaints in the shop. We had somebody come down here not more than a month ago, and he checked everything, the sinks, the bathrooms, the combs, brushes, everything."

I showed him the complaint form and pointed. "You see the

name there, Donald G. Harmon. There's a complaint against the building." I gave him a pained look. "I didn't say that it was against your shop."

"What's it about?" the barber asked.

"Sir, I have to discuss that with the landlord."

"All right, I'll go get him," the barber said. He casually sauntered toward the door, and when I followed him, he stopped. "You better wait here."

"He lives upstairs, doesn't he?" I said matter-of-factly.

"Yeah, he works nights, and maybe he won't like getting awakened so early in the morning. I'll see if he's in and if he wants to talk to you."

My objective was to get inside the building. "Listen, I've got a lot of work to do in this neighborhood today. I can't afford to take time while he decides whether or not he wants to talk to me."

The barber said, "He's the landlord, and I don't like to get him mad. Why don't you wait here? Have a seat, read a magazine."

He went out. Then a curious thing happened. The lottery writer got up from his desk, humming a few bars from *Traviata*, sauntered casually to the street window and pulled the amber sunshade which was halfway drawn all the way down to the bottom.

Within a few minutes, two guys in a Lincoln double-parked, observed the drawn shade and drove off. A van slowed almost to a halt in front of the shop and then took off. The lottery writer jumped to his feet, intercepted a player on the sidewalk and issued a terse warning, and the player departed quickly.

The barber came back. "He's outside waiting for you."

Donald G. Harmon was about sixty-five, tall, thin and wore thick glasses. He knew nothing about any complaints that had been made by any of the tenants in the building. His reaction to the complaint that the Board of Health had received, that there was a terrible stench in the hallways was one of pure astonishment.

"You mean somebody called in and said that? Who? What's his name?"

I became sympathetic. "We get it all the time. Cranks call in, and they're afraid that the landlord is going to give them a hard time if he learns who they are and so they don't leave their names." I waved the complaint form. "But he gave your name and I have to check it out and make a report. I know it's a nuisance, but I have to do it, and the quicker I get it over with, the better it'll be."

"Sons of bitches! You know what they're paying me upstairs, nothing. They're practically living rent free. I'd like to find out who complained." He stared at me as though I knew the culprit's name. His body blocked the buzzer when he pressed it. There was an answering buzz. "Come on," he said angrily, pushing the door open.

There were four apartments on the ground level. Eight on the second and eight on the third. I looked and listened for signs of a lottery operation, telephones ringing, people walking in and out of apartments. On the second floor I heard a woman scolding a child, and that was it. Somewhere behind those doors there was a lottery drop, and as far as finding it, I had nothing to go on.

"I'm sorry if I caused any inconvenience for you. There is no odor in the halls, and I see no violations."

"I could have told you that before we even started. But what the hell, you've got a job to do."

We stood in the downstairs hallway. "Thank you for being so understanding," I said. Police work is a painstaking job, and there are times when you just have to chip away for the next step. "I wouldn't blame you if you called the Board of Health and complained about all this."

His eyes told me that he wasn't about to do that. "No, I'm going to forget the whole thing."

"Thank you again," I said contritely. I had to gain his confidence. "I'd feel better if you'd allow me to buy you breakfast. It would make me feel better. I mean, because of the trouble I've given you."

He smiled, pleased. "No, that isn't necessary."

"You know something, if this type of thing happens again, I'm going to leave my job. I mean, it stinks."

He appeared sympathetic. "No, I wouldn't do that. You've got a city job. You got some security. What makes you think it would be any better somewhere else? Same bullshit wherever you go."

"No, I mean it. Look at how high prices are. I've got a wife and four kids and a house. The mortgage is enough to flatten you every month. My wife is always buying clothes."

He nodded and said nothing, waiting for me to leave. The conversation was over as far as he was concerned.

"I'd have nothing if I left. Do you have a wife?" I asked.

He took his time answering. "No, not now. She died five years ago. I live alone."

"I'm sorry. I was just trying to make conversation."

"That's all right."

"You know what it is. I've been up and down this neighborhood, and you walk around all day and all you see is strangers, and when you walk into a place, they hate you. They think first off that you're going to give them a violation. The job's a bore." I winked. "But once in a while it has its bonuses."

Interest flickered in his eyes. "Yeah, like what?"

"Well, you know how it is. You're always going into stores and apartments and buildings and you meet people."

He grinned. "You talking about broads?"

"I don't gamble, I don't smoke, and I don't drink. For me it's women." I paused while he thought it over. My voice lowered. "There's a joint no more than three blocks away from here."

His glance was sharp. "Where is it? If there is a whorehouse around here, I'd like to know about it."

"You interested because you want to know about it or because you want to get some action?"

"They got anything halfway decent over there?" he said quietly.

"There's two girls. There's a young one who's jerky. She chews bubble gum while she's getting laid, and that turns me off. The other one, Marge, now that's a different story. Did you ever hear of a thirty-three-year-old nymphomaniac whore?"

He stared at me with a faraway look in his eyes. "A nymphomaniac in a whorehouse. No shit?"

His face told me that it was a dream come true for him.

"Look, if you want it, I can set it up for you. The only thing is you can't tell anybody about it. They're very careful. I'll have to tell her about you first." I smiled conspiratorially. "If I tell her you're okay, then you're in."

"Good deal." He was beaming. "Listen, you got a phone number where I can reach you?"

Phone numbers would take away my reason for coming back. "I'd rather not give it out. You never know when somebody's going to pick up a phone and listen in."

He looked dismayed. "Well, how am I going to know?"

"I'll go over there this afternoon, and I'll come back to tell you how I made out."

I pointed at the door. "How do I get in here? I tried buzzing before, and nobody answered." I pointed to the wire going down to the lock release. "That's quite a system. I'd like to have one like that on my front door." I smiled reassuringly. "Is there any special signal that I have to use?"

"You know what it is. The people in the building are afraid that outsiders can get in. So I put the system in. We've got an agreement that nobody gives out the number of times you have to ring the bell. I'll be in the barbershop all afternoon."

It was a disappointment. I wanted to get inside the building, but I sensed that this was not the time to press. "All right, I'll be back."

"I'll be looking for you. When I see you, I'll come right out," he said.

I left him standing on the sidewalk in front of the shop, went back to my car and drove off. I gave myself two hours in which to get back to the shop. The idea was to get my foot in the door back at the lottery operation. I had a plan. Now the trick was to lure Donald G. Harmon to a prostitute, thereby enabling me to gain access to the building. It was going to take some planning. The ideas can come driving around. I drove over to Howard Street. It was still morning, and already the whores and pimps and dope addicts were out sitting on doorsteps, standing in front of bars. They regarded me hatefully. I'd busted half of them. A prostitute who recognized me leered at me scornfully and hobbled away with her syphilitic gait into the Paradise Bar. It was a misnomer. It was filled with diseased, pathetic whores. A junkie staggered over to a nearby wall and vomited. A young whore standing beside him was splattered. She didn't know or didn't care. My stomach turned. They were killing themselves in front of my eyes.

I got out of there. I'd seen enough. I'd planned on lunch before returning to the barbershop. The cup of coffee that I stopped for at a nearby restaurant was as bitter as the taste that remained in my mouth. So much for lunch.

Harmon was waiting for me and completely at ease when I got back to the barbershop. We spoke on the sidewalk.

"I saw her," I said, "and told her about you and it's okay. The only thing is that there's a little problem."

"What is it?" he asked quickly.

"It isn't something that can't be worked out," I explained. "She says that things are bad where she works. She thinks somebody tipped the police off, because she's spotted them watching the house and a couple of them actually came up to the door and rang the bell and said they were sent over by other customers. It's got her and her girlfriend scared crapless. She says her place is too hot and just crawling with police. She stopped operating out of there. She only uses the apartment to sleep in. But she's still working." I grinned at Harmon. "She only takes jobs that require her to go to a customer's home. She won't let anybody near her apartment because she's sure it's being watched. I don't know how you feel about that, but I told her that you wouldn't mind if she came to your place, and she said she'd make it around three or three thirty tomorrow."

"She wants to come here?" He wasn't sure about that. A prostitute could be followed. It was certain that he knew about the lottery operation in the building. Trouble with a prostitute could bring bigger trouble right into his backyard.

There are times when you have to gamble. "Listen, if you have any doubts, then just forget about it. She thinks she's doing me a big favor by coming over here for you. In the sack she's good, and she knows she's good. The fact is that she's very particular about who she screws for. She's run into some weirdos, and if she even suspects that you'd be that way, she won't do it for you."

I saw the light dawn in his eyes. "What the hell do you mean, weirdo?" he asked angrily.

He knew what I meant, and he was letting me know that the term in no way applied to him. "You know what I mean," I said reassuringly. "There are guys who get their kicks by hitting or beating her and even tying her up so they can do anything they want to her. She doesn't want to have anything to do with sadists."

"Who the hell would want to beat her up? Not me. If she comes over to my place, there's only one thing she's going to get." He broke into a broad grin, made a fist with his right hand and moved his arm back and forth. "That's what she gets."

"That's all she wants. I told you that she was a nymphomaniac, didn't I?"

"Send her over. Tell her to hit the buzzer three short and one long and I'll come down and let her in." The story about her being particular had clouded his judgment.

I laughed out loud. "Three shorts and a long. The Morse code or something?"

"Nah! There's an automatic release upstairs that opens the door catch when it receives that signal. You just tell her that I'm an all right guy and send her over."

It was a clever arrangement that he had installed. The building was in a high crime area. People are very nervous these days. Learning the right combination from the tenants would have been very difficult.

I decided that further prying could do no good. He was delighted that Marge would see him tomorrow at the appointed hour, and I let it end like that. I left.

I could have had a policewoman make the necessary purchases for me, but if I brought her in, then it was likely she would have wanted in on my plans. She might have worked out.

She would have been the logical choice for the job. My ego might have had something to do with it, but I was sure that I was a better choice for the part. Because of the decision, I had to be the one to purchase the necessary props.

I drove over to Market and Broad, then walked to a group of specialty shops and went into a dress shop.

A nice young woman in a tight black short dress came forward to greet me. She had pale blond hair and a friendly smile. "Yes, may I help you?"

"Maybe. It could be a problem. I want to buy a dress for my cousin, the problem is that she's overseas."

"Oh, that could be a problem." She seemed disappointed. "Wait a minute. Do you happen to know her height and weight?"

"As a matter of fact, I do," I said. "She's about my size, and weighs about a hundred and fifty-five."

"Oh, she's about five-nine."

"That's it," I said, smiling. "She's exactly my size."
her glance was speculative, and then her face underwent a radical change. She looked uneasy. How could a rugged-looking guy like this with a bashed-in nose and a lantern jaw be a queen of the May? She permitted herself a tiny smile. "I guess you could try it on, and if it fit. . . ." She could hardly wait for me to leave so she could tell the rest of the sales help about it.

"Enough," I said and flashed my shield. "I'm with the vice squad, and I need a dress for a job I'm on." Let them know they're dealing with the police, and suddenly everybody is on a different wavelength.

"Oh," she said in a subdued tone.

I leaned toward her and whispered, "There's fifty white slavers that have come to Newark. You know the type of thing. They get a girl drunk or slip her some knockout drops in her drink and the next thing she finds herself in some room getting raped by a professional rapist. There are guys who get paid for that; most of them wear black patent leather shoes, the narrow pointed kind. Afterward they keep her chained up, probably to a bed, or radiator and the next thing she's shipped out to Las Vegas, or Hong Kong, or even Schenectady."

She looked me right in the eye. "Do you know something, friend? You're full of beans." Then she broke into a wide smile. There's something to be said for Women's Liberation. Once you were able to con them. Today you get back talk.

"Right," I said, "but I do need the dress."

"For a job," she echoed.

I nodded. "An appropriate dress for a hooker is what I need."

She arched an eyebrow. "Streetwalker, call girl, or just plain bedroom floozie?" She was enjoying herself.

"Nothing gaudy. I wouldn't want to get stopped on the street by another cop."

"I've got just the thing. It's last year's and reduced for clearance."

"Long sleeves, high neck?"

"Of course. That would be necessary." And she hurried off toward a stockroom in back.

Watching her, thinking about what I was doing, I grinned at my own expense. I was David Toma, about to play the part of an oversexed hooker. Like they say, you can hardly find any of them anymore.

She brought the dress back. It was one piece with a black top and a flaming red satin skirt. She looked mischievous. "Whorish enough for your taste?" She pointed to the tag. "Thirty dollars, but we'll never sell it. It'll cost you five, if you take it."

Donald G. Harmon was expecting a prostitute. A garish dress could be part of the package. "I'd like to try it on."

"There's a dressing room in back," she said, pointing.

It was a little tight around the waist, but if I tucked myself in, I could manage. I brought it out front and said, "Fine. I'll take it."

She shook her head, laughing. "What's it like?"

"It's a job. If I didn't like what I was doing, I wouldn't do it."

She nodded her head in sober agreement. "Yes, that's what I thought."

I locked the dress in the trunk of my car and drove back to the precinct and went through the book marked Known Gamblers, and could not find the name Donald G. Harmon. It can happen like that, but it doesn't usually. It's a fact that more than 70 percent of all arrests are made on known criminals. The truth is that criminals such as bank robbers, thieves, con men, murderers, smugglers, blackmailers, pimps and corrupt political hacks rarely learn by their mistakes. It was also possible that Harmon was a newcomer to the business.

CHAPTER FIVE

I headed for home. In the morning I was back at the bureau trying to catch up on desk work. I was there for three hours making out affidavits, six petitions for search warrants and an investigator's activity report and time summary. There was a heading for "Offense or activity" in the first column, and under it prostitution, adultery, fornication, unlawful use of narcotics, unlawful possession of narcotics, failure to register as an addict, selling goof-balls, possession of goof-balls, violation of liquor laws, bookmaking, gambling, cards, dice, possession or sale of lottery, warrants served, patrol and observation of others, office detail, court. Under preliminary investigation there were three columns headed activities, hours, arrests and the same headings under followup investigation. Police procedure work can be dull. But there are times when you're doing surveillance in 5 degree temperature when you wish you were back at your desk with the paper work. Today the sun was shining and the weather was mild. By noon I hadn't caught up, but I had made a sizable dent in the work. I was glad to get out of there.

I drove five miles to La Belle Beauty Parlor. I put the car on a private lot behind the shop and went in, carrying my carton containing the dress.

La Belle was Claire Burns and an almost ex-hooker. It happened four years ago at a bar in East Orange. She sat two barstools away and picked up a guy in such bumbling fashion that I knew she had to be an amateur. On the parking lot I told the guy to get lost and sat her down in my car. She was terribly frightened. She thought she was going to be arrested and wept and begged me not to do it. Her explanation was that her husband had deserted her. She had a child at home, the rent was two months late, and she had no one to turn to. It's easy to be cynical after you've arrested many prostitutes. You've heard her story before. I believed her because of her amateurish behavior in the bar. She told me that she was a beautician and hadn't been able to find a job.

"All right, let's see what we can do," I said, and we drove off.

"You're going to arrest me," she said and broke into tears again.

"No, relax, we're going to a beauty shop." Larry Della Russo is a guy who owes me a favor. He also owns five beauty shops. I explained that I had a friend who needed employment.

"Okay," he said, "but she has to be good." Nothing was said to him about what she had tried in the bar. I brought her in to meet him. He questioned her for a while, and then I took her home. Up until the time when we stood outside her three-room apartment I was certain that she had been expecting a pass. She turned the key in the lock, pushed the door open and waited for the expected pitch.

"See you around," I said, and walked away.

When I was halfway down the hall I heard her say, "Thanks," quietly and then the sound of the door closing.

In the morning she went to work. Shortly after, Larry called me and told me that she knew her stuff and was learning more every day. She stayed there for two years, saved some money, and a year later opened her own shop. Bread on the waters. Why not? I took a little satisfaction there.

Claire Burns was taking cash from one of her clients at the register up front. When she finished, she glanced up, saw me, gave a delighted cry and then came running. "Where have you been? I haven't seen you in a dog's age."

"Around, Ma'am, traveling along the Chisholm Trail."

She peered at the dress box. "You going through that female impersonation bit again."

I nodded.

"Coffee? It's just made."

"Can't. I'm late."

She looked disappointed. "You never come around."

I promised that I would.

"You'd better," she said, and gave me the key to her office. I started to go there, and she said, "Come here, you," and when I went to her she kissed me and said, "Drop around. Leave the key on the desk and the door open when you're ready to leave. So long, David." It was a procedure we both knew.

I'd used her office to apply makeup on numerous occasions. What made her office attractive was that it had a door which led to the parking lot. I opened and locked the office door after me and went to work before a wall mirror. Disguising yourself as a woman for a daylight job can be a difficult task. A beard still shows through makeup in daylight. At night along a darkened street or in a bar or alley it's not as obvious. Trying to pass as a prostitute helped. It allowed me to apply a heavy quantity of

93

pancake makeup and eye shadow to the point of grotesquerie. I studied my reflection in the mirror. A cheap-looking hooker could get away with it.

Mastering the disguise of a prostitute had taken months of work. I'd practiced mannerisms in front of a mirror at home, and had used a tape recorder for proper voice and word inflection. I'd studied the actions of hookers. Speed became important. In time I learned to change into other less complicated disguises within 45 seconds.

Harmon wasn't expecting a beauty contest winner. A nymphomaniac hooker was what he eagerly awaited. He was going to see me, a reasonable facsimile. I didn't think that he was especially bright. I looked at myself. I would pass as a hooker. Perhaps I wouldn't to a guy who took a clinical objective gander, but I definitely would pass to an old guy with poor vision who wanted to climb into bed. I left the key, went wobbling on chunky heels to my car and drove out to the barbershop on Hawthorne.

My reflection in the window glass of the door leading to the apartment above the shop gave me a moment when I had to suppress laughter. I didn't really know Donald Harmon, and I didn't know what his taste in prostitutes ran to. In any event Harmon was about to see me. I hit the buzzer three short and a long, and the device inside tripped the lock mechanism. I pushed the door open and went in.

Harmon was standing at the head of the stairs on the second floor with a big welcoming grin, eagerly awaiting the goodies in store for him. I went upstairs, smiled, and in a voice several octaves higher than my own asked if he was Mr. Harmon.

"That's me, baby."

I blinked my eyelids. "A friend of mine told me that you were interested in seeing me."

"I sure am." He jerked a thumb over his shoulder. "My apartment is right down the hall. Why don't we go in there so we can talk privately?"

"Do you mind if we talk here for a while?"

He glanced about nervously as though anticipating one of the tenants interrupting us. "It'll be better if we're out of the hall."

Control is the name of the game. I wanted time in the hallway to spot the apartment that the lottery writer or the barber were using as a drop.

I made a great pretense of studying Harmon. There are few things that will cloud a man's judgment like the prospect of sex with a prostitute. It destroys his logical thinking process. A man interested in a prostitute can readily become a fool and a good vice cop knows it for a fact. The prostitute herself calls her client a "trick" because she reasons that she has tricked him out of his money and she also regards him as a fool. Sex was the common ground for both of us. It allowed us to communicate, and it lulled him into a sense of false security.

I said, "I don't know you, and before I go into a man's apartment, I want to know something about him."

"Listen, you got nothing to be afraid of," Harmon said reassuringly.

"I've heard that before," I said. "A girl can't be too careful. I went into a man's apartment one time and he looked harmless and once we were inside that soon changed." I glanced away as though the memory were too painful for me to recall.

The approach can evoke a certain type of curiosity. Harmon was no exception. "What happened?"

"It makes me uncomfortable just talking about it."

"Come on," Harmon said. "I'm not going to tell anybody."

There is an axiom about a man who is interested in a prostitute, that the more bizarre her activities, the more readily he will believe them. As he listens he becomes more excited and more interested in direct proportion to the story's absurdity. Eventually it can reduce him to a state of idiocy.

I said, "Well, you're not going to believe this, but he made me get down on all fours, and he forced me to crawl around the bedroom like that."

"You're kidding," Harmon said. He sounded disappointed. "I mean making you do that is bad, but I expected to hear worse."

You give them what they want to hear. "I can't, I can't," I said. I gave him a searching glance. "Are you sure you won't repeat this?"

"Of course not, why should I?"

I stared at the floor and lowered my voice. "He painted my fanny red."

"He what?" Harmon asked in an incredulous tone.

Now I looked up. I was trying for the Academy Award. "Yes, he did that to me, and I had to stand still for it while he did it. Otherwise he said that he was going to shoot my brains out. There have been other things like that," I said. "Some of them even worse. So you can understand why I'm so careful about going to a man's apartment. It can be frightening, just being there alone with him if he's a weirdo. I had a terrible job just getting the paint off."

"Yeah, I can understand that," Harmon said. "But you don't have anything to worry about. I like the old-fashioned way."

"So do I," I said.

Fifteen minutes had passed, and there was still no sign of either the numbers writer or the barber. I stalled for time in the hallway by recounting additional fetishisms and assorted perverted activities that I had witnessed and been part of.

I knew that I had stalled him as long as was possible when he placed his hand on my waist and made a sly effort to drop it to my haunch. I caught his wrist and moved his hand away.

I'd put him off as long as I could. "My girlfriend is downstairs in the car waiting for me. She thinks I'm seeing some girl I know. Let me go downstairs and I'll tell her to leave and come back in two hours." I pinched his cheek lightly and coyly said, "Do you think that will be enough time for you?"

"Two hours will be just right."

"All right. You go back into your apartment so when I come back we won't be seen by anybody going into your place together."

"You won't be too long," he said in an anxious tone.

My goal was to get a glimpse of the numbers drop. "Be patient, honey. It'll be a little while. I have to give her directions to someplace in East Orange, and as soon as I do that, I'll be back."

He waved to me from his door and went in. Downstairs I opened and slammed the front door shut and remained in the hall, waiting. Fifteen minutes went by without any sign of the barber or the numbers writer. I momentarily expected Harmon to come searching for me. When I least expected it, the numbers writer loomed up outside the door. When he pressed the buzzer, I was already climbing the stairs. I gambled that the drop was on the second floor and headed toward Harmon's apartment. I heard the reassuring sounds of his footsteps behind me, and when they stopped, I went directly to Harmon's door and knocked and glanced back casually. The writer stopped at the third door from the top of the stairs. Four sharp raps was the signal. There was a muffled voice from behind the door, and the numbers writer replied, "Yeah, it's Jimmy."

There was the sound of various locks and bolts opening, then the sound of a door chain being released.

97

Harmon shut the door after me. "There's a problem," I said quickly.

My distressed appearance seemed to confuse him. "What's up?"

"Gloria has been having all kinds of trouble. She was just sitting in the car waiting for me and a couple of guys came up to the car trying to make out with her. You're not going to believe it, but they tried to pull her out of the car. Anyway she managed to lock the door and windows, and she frightened them off by honking the horn. She just wants to get out of here. She's excitable. She kept talking about somebody who might have seen what happened to her calling the police."

"No, no, you don't want her doing that," Harmon said.

"I'll tell you what. This thing has got me so upset I won't be worth a damn." I winked at him. "Suppose I come back tomorrow at the same time and I'll come right up to your apartment."

He shrugged. "I would have liked it today, but I can wait."

"How about getting a bottle of Canadian so we can have a few drinks?"

"I got a whole closet filled with booze. I'll see you tomorrow. Only do one thing. Come back yourself tomorrow. Don't bring your girlfriend with you. She sounds like a pain in the ass."

"She is. I'll see you tomorrow, by myself," I said, and left. I removed my shoes and made my way over to the apartment where I'd last seen the numbers writer. The phone rang, and I heard somebody accepting bets. That did it. I traveled the rest of the way barefoot through the hall and down the stairs. I slipped the shoes on behind the street door and went out.

I was satisfied with my progress. I'd gained Harmon's confidence as the Health Inspector. Then while playing the role of prostitute I'd learned the location of the drop, the name Jimmy, and the four sharp rap signal that would open the door. I'd manipulated Harmon so that I could come back tomorrow with reinforcements and easily gain access. We wouldn't have to knock any doors down and we wouldn't allow the operators enough time to destroy evidence. If it went according to my plan it would work.

Back in my car I drove three blocks and found a block of abandoned, partially torn-down buildings. I changed completely into my own clothes, applied cold cream to remove the makeup, went back to the precinct and typed out an affidavit describing what I had observed at the barbershop address and the building which housed it, description and names of those persons illegally involved in the gambling operations and their actions. To obtain a search warrant it is first necessary to fill out an affidavit. This is part of the search and seizure laws. Contrary to a belief held by many that it can hinder and impede justice and arrests, the affidavit, properly drawn and outlining completely what had been observed, can make a more solid case for the prosecution. Years ago I remember Lieutenant Dougherty saying that search warrants, aside from the obvious reasons of protecting the innocent, made the policeman search for the knowledge of the crime rather than go in with a hammer in hand and conceivably come up empty when the case went to court. In short, having to obtain the warrant, made for a better, more intelligent police officer. It's a premise with which I agree.

At the bottom of the affidavit there is a paragraph that begins: "I have just and reasonable cause to suspect and believe, and do suspect and believe that the following goods, memoranda, sheets and property, to wit: slips, papers, records, books and paraphernalia in connection with the crime of Lottery 2A:121-3 and Bookmaking 2A:112-3 are concealed on the persons listed above and also on the premises. I therefore pray that a warrant be issued and said persons be searched as well as the said premises and persons therein."

That's the long and the short of an affidavit. I made it out, brought it to a magistrate for his approval and signature, and he issued a search warrant.

Armed with the warrant and accompanied by six detectives, I returned on the following day. A fast pass revealed that Harmon, the barber and writer were all in the shop. It could have been a tricky operation. Three men were assigned to hit the barbershop and the other half of the team was simultaneously to hit the upstairs apartment. If the barbershop had an electrical signal button, then the operators in the upstairs apartment could be tipped off. It could also work the other way. Slips could be flushed down toilets or burned or swallowed. Pails are deliberately kept filled for slips that are water-soluble.

We synchronized our watches and gave ourselves five minutes to hit both operations. The smart cop knows that a criminal can recognize a detective often more readily than he can recognize a criminal. We approached from the blind side so that we wouldn't have to pass before the barbershop's window. I stood before the door myself, hit the button three shorts and a long, and when the answering buzz came back, I pushed the door open and Nicosia, Powers and Beckerman darted into the hallway. The other plainclothesmen were off the street and out of sight. It was my job, and it was done my way. I didn't want three detectives sitting in plain sight in an unmarked car. The three detectives were down on the floor of the car. Take three husky guys in business suits sitting in a car, and there's a strong chance that a suburban schoolboy is going to recognize them as cops, let alone a lookout if there was one in the area. In the hallway we removed our shoes. Earlier, preparing for the hit, Nicosia had mumbled something about his new shoes and that he was going to kill anyone who stole them. Whereupon Beckerman remarked that he wouldn't be caught dead wearing suede faggot shoes and that anyone who stole them had to be sick. Nicosia had replied, "Balls."

I rapped four times sharply on the door. Nicosia and Beckerman stood to my right out of sight. A voice behind the door called, "That you, Jimmy?"

"Yeah, it's Jimmy," I replied.

There was the sound of several locks being opened. When the door opened a crack, I spotted the door chain. I hit the door with my shoulder ripping the chain off and hitting the man behind it. The impact knocked the man to the floor. Nicosia, Powers and Beckerman, with guns drawn, came storming in behind me. There were four startled operators seated at the telephones.

The man on the floor was silent, too upset to question anyone's authority. His expression was one of total disbelief. He was told to get to his feet. The operators were put into handcuffs and informed of their rights by Nicosia while the rest of us went through the apartment. There were five telephones. We confiscated $3,500 in cash, $8,000 in lottery plays, three handguns and a shotgun. When I went downstairs, the barber, the writer and Harmon were already cuffed. I was unrecognized without my disguises.

Kippler grinned and showed me a fistful of paper slips. "There's hundreds of dollars here," he said.-

I said, "Who owns the building?"

Harmon frowned. "I do."

"Let's go upstairs," I said. "I want to take a look at your apartment. I've got a search warrant," I said and showed it to him. The apartment was clean, but he had to know there was gambling on the premises.

We brought them in and booked them. I went to Don's Diner with Nicosia for coffee and spent an hour unwinding.

It was 9 P.M. when I turned the key in the lock. Pat was waiting for me in the kitchen. When you live with a person long enough, words aren't always necessary.

I said, "What happened, Pat?"

She didn't answer.

"Come on, Pat, what's wrong?"

"There was another one of those phone calls. It didn't start as an obscene call, but it ended that way. It was a man asking for you. I told him that you weren't home and asked if he wanted to leave a message or his name. He said to tell you that you were getting too ambitious and that if you know what's good for you, you'll lay off the lottery banks. He said stop playing hero, and that they're going to chop you up so bad there won't be anything left to carry off to the morgue."

"Did you say anything to him?"

"Nothing. I was so frightened I was numb."

"It's all right, Pat."

It was an awkward moment for her. She seemed apologetic. "David, he told me what he was going to do to me. Then he said that I had nice kids and I wouldn't like it if anything happened to them."

I held her in my arms. "Oh, David," she said. "He frightened me."

CHAPTER SIX

In the morning on the way to the precinct I detected a blue Dodge with Pennsylvania license plates in the rearview mirror. He was following me, and it took about two miles before it registered. The phone call to my wife had something to do with it. It had kept me awake for hours. I'd checked Jimmy, Donna, Patty Anne and Janice four times. I'd awakened feeling apprehensive. All threats are not necessarily idle. Violence does not always occur instantaneously. I'd been doing a good job on the lottery drops and banks. Hit organized crime in the pocket where it counted often enough, and there was a good chance that it would strike back at the source of its problem. But both sides knew the rules. Hitting a man through his family wasn't one of them. That way it becomes a form of blackmail, and when it occurs, you suspend the rules and make your own.

I caught three traffic lights en route to the Garden State Parkway. The man in the Dodge deliberately slowed and pulled toward the curb so that another car would be the one directly behind me. When the light changed, I got over to the right, circled the block and viewed him in the mirror again. I pulled in at a body and fender shop, got out of the car without glancing back and walked over to the door of the office. Opening it, I glimpsed the blue Dodge double-parked half a block away. I went inside to stall for a minute.

There was an old man in coveralls behind the battered desk. He said, "Yeah, can I help you?"

"I'm looking for Pete Langer."

"Pete who?"

"Langer. I think he works here."

"No." He shook his head. "We got nobody here by that name."

"Sorry," I said and walked out. I went back to the car and drove off. He stuck like a leech. I almost lost him when he was stopped by a light at University and Market. I slowed by getting behind a garbage truck, allowing him time to catch up. I was leading and didn't want to lose him. After the threats on the phone there was the possibility that someone had chosen him to do a job on me.

I considered driving up to the precinct, going inside for a minute and having one of the boys tail the Dodge. He might not be there when I came out. Proximity to a police station could make him very nervous.

I drove down Market Street. There were some buildings that would have suited my purpose. The street was parked solid with cars and trucks. I remembered an office building on a quiet lateral street. I'd made a narcotics pinch on the third floor two years ago. It was both a factory and office building. The tail was a few seconds behind when I made the right turn. I parked, and he drove past and chose a spot up ahead. I gave him enough time to pick me up again by pretending to study the contents of a brown manila envelope before I got out of the car.

The hunter knew what he was doing. He crossed to the other side of the street. He was a small man in a tweed coat and scarf and a plaid all-weather hat. He had a pencil-thin mustache and an old-style brown leather briefcase. To all outward appearances he was an ordinary type of man.

The briefcase bothered me. That could house a large variety of deadly weapons. He was an inconspicuous man. The thought occurred that if he was in the business of knocking somebody off, he could walk in and out of town without attracting a second glance.

I went into the building and studied the lobby directory. He remained outside on the sidewalk. I ignored the self-service elevator and headed for the service stairs. We all have our little idiosyncrasies. I become claustrophobic in elevators. If my pursuer wanted to know where I was headed, he was going to have to climb stairs.

I ascended quietly and heard him on the second flight. The fact that he was following me that closely was enough for me. He figured to be a specialist. If they were going to pick a guy to work me over with his fists, they would have chosen a guy with hands like rocks, a guy big enough to knock me down.

They'd picked a little guy with a briefcase. Small guy, big gun. Will travel and work cheap. It could work like that. He could be fast, good enough to do the job. There could be a silencer on the gun. I made noise climbing the stairs. He was closing the distance between us.

He was still out of sight. I stopped for a second, and he took a few more stairs and stopped when he realized what had happened. When I got to the next landing, I knew the way I wanted it handled. I drew my gun, flipped the cylinder open, removed one bullet and slipped it into my pocket. I made certain that he heard me opening and shutting the door to the third floor. It opened outward into the landing. Nobody was in the hallway. A good-sized din came from a small printing plant.

I leaned back against the wall and aimed my gun at about midsection height in case he came in crouching. It could be a very quick business.

There was a sound behind the door. He stepped into the hall. I saw no gun. He looked to the left first; then when he turned his head to the right, I hit him with my fist. He had a split second to see it coming, and he jerked his head back. He hurtled down the hall, sliding on his back. He fell apart, hat, briefcase and himself traveling in different directions. Noises reverberated in the hallway, but nobody came out to see what was going on. It seems to be a sign of the times. A little noise in the hall. Maybe somebody is getting mugged. Just keep the door closed and mind your own business. That way you'll never get hurt. But sometimes it can be the other way around, when it's you out in the hallway.

My hunter was asleep. He lay there in an undignified heap, with a smear of blood at the side of the mouth. Blood stained his shirt collar and tie. I patted him down and took a .25 Beretta automatic from his shoulder holster and a wallet from his rear pants pocket and dropped them into my jacket pocket. The briefcase was a prop. All it held was a map of New Jersey. Somebody had printed directions to my house, including a diagram of how the streets were laid out at the bottom over the mileage scale. I stuck the map in my pocket, returned my gun to its holster. I placed my hand under his armpits and dragged him into the men's room. He owed me an explanation. He groaned, opened his eyes and recognized me as his assailant. He made a grab for his gun, which was no longer there. For a man coming out of induced sleep he was very quick. He scrambled to all fours and lunged forward at my legs with outstretched arms as though trying to make a tackle on the three-yard line. I stepped out of his way.

"Try it again, Mustache, and I'll throw you out the window," I said.

He glared at me, touching his jaw gingerly.

I removed the map from my pocket without taking my eyes off him. "You've got directions to my house and you've been tailing me. Why?"

"You shouldn't have hit me like that. I was just doing my job." I was just doing my job. It's an overworked phrase.

I drew my gun. I'd had enough. The events of the last two days stuck in my throat. "On your back, bum."

He looked at my face, turned pale and stretched out on the floor. I stood straddling him and pointed a gun between his eyes. "What job? Kill my family? Me? Who do you start with?"

"I don't want to kill anybody," he said in a hoarse, strained voice. "A guy hired me to follow you and report on your activities, and that's all there was to it."

"Who hired you? Where do you come off tailing somebody? Who the hell are you?" Talking to him brought a vivid picture of my wife weeping last night after she had received the phone call.

"I'm a private investigator." He spoke quickly. "A guy came in and told me what he wanted. He paid me heavy bread, well over what I thought the job was worth. So I took it."

"What's with this private detective crap?"

"I've got a card. It's in my wallet. It's in my pocket," he stammered.

I stepped away from him. "Stay right there. Don't move." There was a card for a private investigator in the Commonwealth of Pennsylvania and a name, Henry T. Baldwin. There was a driver's license, a Social Security card, a pistol permit, and a photograph of him with a dark-haired woman. I removed his photograph and showed it to him. "Is this your wife?"

"Yes."

"If I don't hear what I want to hear, you'll never see her again."

"I'm telling you all there is," he said. He appeared more bewildered than frightened.

I said, "Do you know who I am?"

"All I got was a name, David Toma, and an address."

"You're full of shit. They'd have to tell you that I was a cop."

"Yes, yes, they did."

"Who are they?"

He sighed. "There was one man, Charlie Zhadrool. That was it."

"Charlie Zhadrool?"

"Yes, that was it."

"Do you know what that means?" I asked.

"I don't understand."

"Zhadrool, it means Cucumber, in Italian. So maybe you think I want to play games with you?"

"No, I don't think that. There was a guy in a tan Buick with Jersey plates. That much I know. I saw the car."

"Did you get his license number?"

"No. For what reason?"

"How much did he pay you?"

"Five hundred, all cash. So help me, he gave me the name Charlie Zhadrool. I knew he was lying, but I didn't care. It was maybe two days' work. I figured I'd drive over, spend a couple of nights and drive on back home. Honest, that's all there was to it. Listen, I'm a family man."

"Your office is across the state line. Didn't you think it was unusual for somebody to come to you from out of state with a tailing job in Newark?"

He was beginning to regain his composure. "In my business I'm used to all sorts of strange requests. It's why people go to private investigators in the first place."

"How long have you been a licensed investigator, Mr. Baldwin?"

"Fifteen years." His pale, washed-out eyes searched my face as though to anticipate what I was driving at.

"That's a long time. I'd say that a man should know his business in fifteen years." I smiled at him reassuringly.

He smiled for the first time, cagily. He was beginning to feel a little more at ease. He sat up, and I didn't stop him.

I said, "A guy comes to you from out of state, gives you a joke name, tells you he wants a guy tailed in another state, and you go along with it. You really get strange requests in your business."

"Yes, of course, I get them all the time."

"How about a request for setting somebody up? Did you ever think of that?"

If he had, his expression didn't tell me. He was still too much in control. He wasn't ready to do any good for me. I said, "Did it ever occur to you that if somebody turned the lights out for me that maybe he'd come back and do the same for you? You don't even know his real name. How could you protect yourself? You wouldn't know who to look out for."

The thought hadn't occurred to him, and now that it had, his face underwent a sudden change. Fear drained it of color. "You're putting me on."

"Give me one good reason," I said, and waited. "I want his description, make of car. You said a Pontiac?"

He smiled. "No, I said a Buick. He was a big guy, about six three, I'd say."

"Hair, eyes, distinguishing marks, mannerisms, speech. What was he wearing?"

He stared off, pretending to recollect. "He was tall, and his hair was kind of dirty blond, sandy-colored, you know what I mean?"

I nodded as though I did. "What else?"

"Well, I think his eyes were blue or gray. They could have been either color. I'm not sure."

My mild-appearing man was lying. "That's good," I said. "What else can you tell me?"

"There was something odd. I had the feeling that he had a game leg."

"He was lame?"

"Maybe yes, maybe no. He walked very slowly when he came into my office, as though he were favoring his right leg."

"And maybe he had a patch over his eye and a small case of hives. That description matches nobody that I know," I said.

"That may be, but what can I do about that?"

I was tired of his lies. I waved my gun and aimed it at his head. "I'll tell you what you can do about that. You can give me a description of a guy that I know."

"Suppose I don't know anybody like that?" he asked quietly.

"Then you've got a lot of trouble."

"Come on, be reasonable. I told you what the guy looked like."

I grinned at him. "I don't know anybody with that description." I broke the gun apart, spun the cylinder, removed five bullets and showed them to him. "Do you know how many bullets there are in this gun?" I asked.

"Six."

"That's correct." I flipped the cylinder shut. "It means there's one left. Now let me lay it out the way I see it. I went to this building, and I saw no one, and I doubt that anyone saw me. Right?"

He didn't answer.

"Now I'm going to start pulling the trigger. One shot at a time. Like Russian roulette. If you're lucky, maybe you get a chance or two. Real lucky and you get five chances."

"Come on, will you? You've got to be kidding. You mean you're going to kill me because I was tailing you?"

"I've been getting threats over the phone. My wife listened to a filthy animal threatening me and herself and my kids."

"I didn't have anything to do with that. The worst kind of an animal would do that."

"You really don't understand," I said. "You don't think that I'll do it."

"Please, I'm telling you what the man looked like. What more can I do? Listen, I've got three kids at home. Honest, mister, I don't know anything about anybody wanting to set you up." His fear had drained the blood from his face. I couldn't tell which of his fears was greater, for those who had hired him or his fear of me. The latter had to be the greater. He had to believe that he was going to die here and now.

I waved the muzzle of the gun and aimed it at a point two inches to the right s head. "I don't want to kill you. It won't give me any pleasure. But if that's the way you want it, then that's the way it's going to be," I said. I turned the gun to his head and pulled the trigger. It hit with a sharp, metallic sound.

"Please, please, have a heart." His jaw worked, and I watched tears form in his eyes. "I don't want to die. For God's sake, man, what are you doing to me?"

I heard the words in a thin whine, and they were the wrong

words. It would be ironic if he were telling me the truth. He was such a meek little guy. I was beginning to wonder if he had the nerve to lie with a gun pointed at his head.

I pulled the trigger again and the firing pin hit on another empty chamber.

He gagged and held a hand to his mouth. His color was poor. "All right, all right. Put the gun away. I'll tell you what you want to know." His eyes moved about wildly. "Don't, don't do anything." The words were a broken sound.

"Give me his name."

"Honest, honest to God. I don't know."

I believed him. The time for lying had passed for him. I said, "Describe him."

"If I tell you and it gets back to him, I'm as good as dead. That's the feeling I've got about that guy."

"Is it the same kind of feeling you got when you took the five hundred to set me up?"

He didn't answer.

It had to be now. "You're dead right now, if you don't tell me what I'm expecting to hear."

He nodded and spoke very slowly. "The name he gave me was Charlie Zhadrool. I knew he was lying. I didn't want to take the case when he came into my office. It smelled. I knew he'd come too far to hire somebody he wanted tailed in Newark."

"But you took it."

"Yes. I even asked him about it. He said that he wanted me to do the job because he was well known in Newark and there was always a chance that a Newark investigator would leak information out and that would be embarrassing for him."

"Describe him to me," I said.

"He's a big guy, wears a cheap toupee. There's a scar on his neck that his collar didn't hide completely. He wore dark glasses, and he's got a nervous habit, he keeps clearing his throat while he's talking to you."

I'd heard enough. The man he had described was Paul Perault. Perault worked for a mobster named Freddie Casatelli.

I removed the bullets from his gun and handed it to him. "Don't come back here again, Baldwin, for any reason." He dropped the gun into his pocket, and I walked him out of there. In the hallway he backed through the door and went to the top of the service stairs without taking his eyes off me. His feet pounded heavily down the stairs. I heard him stumble and fall, and then he was running again. He hadn't violated the law. I had no reason to book him and he wasn't going to complain to anyone.

I went downstairs and drove slowly toward the precinct. There was a vague unrest in the back of my mind. Why would Casatelli bring in a stranger to tail me when he had hoods galore on his payroll who could do it? The answer came back with unexpected swiftness. Casatelli had to assume that I would spot one of his men easily. If I didn't, and they set me up, then there might also be a possibility that a leak could develop. The way he had it planned was to get rid of me, and then he'd take care of the man who'd tailed me. To wipe it completely clean, he'd also have to get rid of Perault. That was a strong possibility because it was rumored that Perault had been playing around with Casatelli's wife. She'd disappeared two months ago.

CHAPTER SEVEN

I went down to the street and thought about Perault and Freddie Casatelli. Perault was a thug, and Casatelli was a top figure in organized crime. Perault and I were both products of the same Newark ghetto. When I went off into the Marines during the Korean War, Perault was doing time in an Illinois correctional institute.

At Parris Island I was awarded a certificate as the outstanding marine in the company. I like to be first in what I do. I compete. They made me a drill instructor, and I wasn't too happy with it. There's a certain cold detachment that goes with the job, but I worried about those kids. They hammer it into you that your rifle is your best friend, and you keep it clean, mister, or they'll walk you twenty miles for not doing it. The discipline is a necessary part of the training. It can save your life; but the power is sometimes abused, and the cruelty can come through as an ugly thing.

Perault thrived on cruelty. When he got out of the correctional institute, he pimped by living off the earnings of two prostitutes. He beat them regularly while playing one against the other with promises of estatelike mansions in the country and matrimony. The prostitutes compared notes and planned revenge. Perault passed out at a drunken orgy, and one of the prostitutes sliced his neck and both hookers lit out for parts unknown with his bankroll.

The scar on his neck and the loss of the money made Perault meaner than he already was. To recoup his losses, he held up a bar and pistol-whipped the bartender after he had already taken his money.

The bartender pursued him into the street shouting for help, and help unexpectedly appeared in the form of a radio patrol car carrying two police officers. Perault made a mad dash. One of the officers fired a shot into the air, and Perault stopped and dropped his gun. The episode earned him a jail sentence of five to ten. At the time of his arrest Perault had an apartment that cost him $500 a month, and there was strong evidence that he was running a muscle protection racket on various storekeepers and tavern owners. There was a belief held by the police that Perault had probably committed forty or more crimes before he was apprehended.

When he returned to the outside world, he was hired by Freddie Casatelli as a collector and muscleman for his loansharking operation. Perault continued to establish his reputation as one who would savagely beat those who didn't make their payments promptly. For Casatelli the loan sharking was a natural outgrowth of his gambling empire. The gambler, the guy who can't stay away from it, is a loser, and a loser is always in to the syndicate, and Freddie had him wrapped up on both ends.

I gave Casatelli lots of thought. He'd threatened my family. Freddie Casatelli, a product of Chicago slums who'd come East to make it big. He'd tried in New York, and the law and the mob had harassed him. So he'd wormed his way into New Jersey. He'd been arrested thirty-three times with one conviction, which was later overturned. Freddie Casatelli, fifty-five years old, the boss of an organized crime ring, specializing in gambling, loan sharking, protection and occasional heroin importing. A very careful man, Casatelli, with legitimate business some of which occasionally ran in the red to be written off as tax losses and used as cover for the more lucrative narcotics importing.

He made an enormous fortune, and when it began to appear that there was no limit on the money to be made from heroin, the government, the FBI, and the Federal Bureau of Narcotics clamped down and sent some of Freddie's friends to penitentiaries for terms of twenty and thirty years. Government agents knew too much about Casatelli, his haunts, associates, movements and activities for him to continue. So Freddie to all outward appearances turned a new leaf and confined his activities to legitimate ventures. But the gambling and the loan sharking continued to flourish, and with amassed money Freddie would take enormous one-shot narcotics-importing deals. He'd taken a bust on a shipment that was discovered on a ship in New York Harbor. Wholesale value was $3,000,000. It was an unpleasantness, but he could live with it.

To insure against the possibility of any involvement, organized crime members limit their activities to the importation and initial distribution of heroin. Thereafter the drug is cut, distributed and diluted even more, depending on the profit wished for, before it reaches the pusher and the addict.

Because of the stiff penalties involved in the narcotics racket, a long chain of command was utilized to protect the top men from arrests that can possibly stem from the testimony of an underling. The Portuguese sailors who had hidden the heroin aboard the ship did not know the two men to whom the heroin was transferred at the pier. None of them knew Casatelli, but it was his money that had set up the operation. Police, FBI, Interpol, and special Narcotics Investigation units know the identity of most narcotic traffickers, but without proof they can't be arrested. Obtaining proof is difficult.

Casatelli still had the third largest gambling operation in northern New Jersey to keep him happy. There are many people today who are of the opinion that since gambling, narcotics and loan sharking are so successful, any reports of organized crime as being involved in legitimate business are highly exaggerated and used solely as a method to increase appropriations for crime-fighting agencies. If anything, crime reports never tell the complete story. Organized crime rarely, if ever, reveals the businesses it has taken over. But organized crime can operate a legitimate business with tremendous advantage by operating in an illegitimate manner. Competitors are intimidated. Manufacturers are advised that they cannot sell certain merchandise to their competitors. Employees are paid less than a union wage. The entire operation can be used as a fence setup, and merchandise purchased at the agreed-upon price for hot goods can be resold at very low prices.

For the racketeer, operating a legitimate business is absolutely essential for his survival in illegal activities. A legal business offers a source of reportable income. A racketeer can't reveal that he earns his living as the head of a call girl operation, or loan shark, narcotics importer, gambling operator, hijacker or receiver of stolen goods. A legitimate business conceals his involvement in crime and gives him respectability as a member of a community.

But the most important reason for this need for legitimate enterprises is that it gives him the opportunity to convert dirty money into clean money. It affords him the opportunity to realize profit from legitimate business instead of deriving it from crime ventures. Payrolls can be padded with hoods and their relatives who draw company salaries for illegal activities that are in no way related to the legitimate business.

Casatelli's putting a tail on me with the obvious purpose of setting me up had to come from the fact that I had proved to be a source of irritation to him. I'd broken five of his number drops and three of his banks where he employed upper-echelon hoods, and all that had brought threatening phone calls to my home.

There's a vast difference between organized crime and street crime. When a burglar, mugger, car thief or con man is arrested and taken out of circulation, it follows that the number of crimes will be fewer than would otherwise be the case. In organized crime, loss of income and personnel that have been arrested rarely destroys the organization. Casatelli would merely replace the personnel and resume gambling operations elsewhere.

Casatelli had the money and the clout to provide the legal expenses for his personnel that I had arrested, and he'd provide for their families. After they did their time, Casatelli would provide a job in the organization, even though it might not be what the convicted gang members had had previously.

Organized crime had bribed arresting officers to reduce charges and had made attempts to bribe district attorneys and judges. To attempt this, the members of organized crime have to know people in still higher positions who will keep them from being arrested if the bribery attempt should fail.

I keep hearing eminent criminologists advancing the theory that the police actually do very little to prevent crimes of violence. They say the police are mainly engaged in victimless crime wars. These are the pearls of wisdom uttered by people who have never been involved in street crime and related offenses.

Street crime is caused by and is the direct result of the existence of organized crime. Most felonies that occur are the direct result of organized crime's importation of hard drugs. An addict can spend $40 to $100 a day on drugs, and to raise the money he steals, cons and hustles. He rarely receives more than 20 percent of the value of the stolen goods. It means that he has to steal as much as $200 to $300 daily to satisfy his craving for the drug. Consider how many addicts there are in the country today, and the importance of organized crime's trafficking in drugs becomes enormous. Organized crime provides the fence necessary to take the hot goods off the junkies' hands. The figures run into billions of dollars drained from the ghetto areas alone. Often welfare checks provided for the slum dweller for his food, rent and clothing find their way into the hands of organized crime. Dope, numbers, lottery and loan sharks eat him up.

He plays numbers out of a sense of desperation, with the thought that if he hits, somehow he'll have enough money to move away from the ghetto. He buys number dream books which supposedly interpret his dreams and provide a number that corresponds to his dreams. If he has a dream about a long-lost relative who visited him and arrived by train he can find listed under relatives numbers for trains, airplanes, horses, arguments, love, sun, sky, moon. There's a number for everything, and it's usually accompanied by a piece of advice: Play this one for three weeks. Often the bookmaker has his own dream book which he will refer to for the benefit of the players. The books are a con. The facts are that the odds against hitting the numbers are 1,000 to 1, but the payoff is 500 and sometimes 600 to 1. With an edge like that the player doesn't have a chance. The proposal that the state take over the numbers game has been met with fierce resistance, as somehow threatening to corrupt the state. It would not corrupt the state, as the lottery did not corrupt the state. The state and its residents would benefit, and enormous revenue would be sheared from organized crime.

The times are strange. To the young slum dweller, top mobsters are often regarded as heroes. On the screen the appearance of pimps driving pimpmobiles is greeted with applause and gleeful shouts. All that the ghetto teaches a delinquent is to grow rich by hustling and not to get caught.

To the slum kid Casatelli was a hero. There's a belief held by some that a racketeer can be a charming, witty, urbane fellow with a great sense of humor, a sort of harmless colorful hood. I know differently. They're disguised thugs.

I was involved with Casatelli. He was capable of the most vicious acts, and they could be enacted against my family and myself. I drove my car back to the precinct lot and got out and walked to an entrance door and stopped for a minute. The full impact of Casatelli had my stomach churning. I had a lot to worry about. Nothing good happens to you of its own accord. Casatelli would ease off only if I forced him off. The idea was not to get killed in the process.

There were cases that I had pending, but it was impossible to concentrate on them because of the threat that Casatelli posed to my family. That could be police business, but I preferred to handle that one on a personal level.

I made three phone calls and spoke to three guys. The first two knew where Freddie Casatelli lived but didn't know where he hung out during the daylight hours. Possibly they did, but

you can't be sure of anything when you're talking to informants. I took a random shot and called Lover Harry. He owed
me a favor. Lover Harry was Harry Boltene, the proprietor of a
topless go-go joint in downtown Newark. He was called Lover
Harry because he made going to bed with him a condition for a
go-go dancer seeking employment with him.

One who had come up from Atlanta and had acceded to his
demands was followed shortly thereafter by her boyfriend, who
visited her one evening while she was performing. At the bar he
heard various comments from the patrons such as, "Well,
there's another one you can chalk up for Lover Harry." Another
commented that the Lover said she really liked it and could
hardly get enough. It gradually dawned upon the boyfriend
that they were talking about the woman he loved. Thereupon
he wanted to know who the hell this Lover Harry was and how
did they know for a fact that the girl dancing had succumbed to
Harry's charm.

It was explained to the boyfriend that Harry's dubious charm
had very little to do with Harry's lovemaking.

"How come?" said the boyfriend.

"How come," said the patrons, "is that if they want to work
for Harry, they have to screw for Harry."

The last comment was met by an outraged cry from the
boyfriend who sprang to his feet, pulled a knife and charged
toward Lover Harry, who was standing at the end of the bar,
leering at the boyfriend's girlfriend.

Fortunately for Lover Harry, I was at the bar doing surveillance on a man suspected of trafficking in cocaine. As the
boyfriend went by, I stuck a foot out and tripped him. It
probably saved Lover Harry's life or, at the very least, saved
him from a nasty slice. It was an act for which Lover Harry was
indeed grateful. I didn't want his gratitude. I wanted informa-

tion on Freddie Casatelli. Lover Harry had go-go dancers who attracted patrons who worked for Casatelli. I'd seen them there.

Lover Harry said, "Yeah, sure I know. He owns a social and fraternal club over in East Orange. It's a real swank joint from what I heard."

I got the address and said, "Do me a favor, Harry. I'd appreciate it if you kept it quiet about my asking."

There was a long silence, and then he said, "Listen, I'm not crazy. I'm not looking for trouble. I owe you. I know who Casatelli is. If anybody even asked me about him, I'd just tell him I never heard of the guy."

I thought of the conditions that he set for employment in his dive. Any day now somebody was going to step in there and slice his ears off. And sooner or later one of the girls was going to make a complaint to the police. I'm a cop, and cops sometimes make deals with the opposition; but if one of his go-go girls ever got over her fright and complained, I'd book him myself.

Back in the car it took me a few minutes to break open my suitcase. I became an auto mechanic dressed in dirty coveralls. I smeared some grease on my hands and a few smudges on my face and slipped a long-haired wig on. I drove toward East Orange to settle my account with Freddie Casatelli. I believe, like some of the old time Italians occasionally referred to as Mustaches, that when a man has a problem he goes directly to the man who created the problem and he ends it, one way or another. I don't believe that you stand still and wait for things to get worse. That way they do.

Casatelli was a powerful mob boss in New Jersey, and he hadn't risen to that position of power on the garbage heap without opposition by those he had dethroned. Casatelli had been fired at three times in his car during assassination attempts. His home had been fire-bombed. Dynamite planted in his Lincoln caused the bizarre death of a car thief attempting to steal it from a parking lot. Casatelli never went anywhere without a bodyguard, and it logically followed that he'd have some kind of protection at the club. He'd be more relaxed in his own surroundings, but protection would be there. There was a good chance that I could have gone to the door, flashed my shield and been ushered in to see him. That would have made it police business, and hoods know that if a detective walks into a place of business, it's likely that other police know his whereabouts. It means that he can walk in and out with relative safety. It can be a deceptive form of self-assurance. The hood might not follow that line of thinking, and even if he did, he could choose to ignore it.

I didn't want to go in as a cop. This was a personal matter that involved Patricia and the kids. I operate with what I know about myself, and it's what makes me most effective. I don't worry about what the next man is supposed to do or think. As the song says, "I've got to be me," and like that I can function.

Casatelli's building was one story high, windowless, of brick, and it had its own parking lot. I found a slot on the next block, removed my gun from its holster, dropped it into a pocket in my coveralls and slid a small wrench into another pocket so that it protruded as a mechanic's prop. I went in swinging my ignition keys without attracting a second glance. There were three pool tables in use and a group of card tables with gambling chips. A quick estimate placed the number of guys in the one big room at about fifty.

The club was lavishly furnished, with thick red carpeting, soft divans, oil paintings on the walls and some statuary, including one of a small boy urinating into a fish tank. I recognized some of the assemblage of murderers, pushers, muscle and protection men. I counted five that I'd arrested. Nobody recognized me. They shot pool and played cards. Paul Perault was at the rear of the room. Behind him, seated on a massive easy chair, I could see Freddie Casatelli, and alongside him I recognized Aldo Simonetti, who was out on bail awaiting trial for armed robbery.

An olive-complected man, resplendent in a dark-blue silk suit, approached. He wanted to know what I was doing there. I said quickly, "I'm dropping a car off. I'm supposed to meet the guy here and give him the keys."

He held his hand out. "I'll give him the keys. Who is he?"

You don't have to answer all the questions. I said, "There's a bill for thirty-five dollars for an alternator. You gonna pay me?"

He glanced at my hands. "All right, stick around. Don't touch anything."

"I'm not going to touch anything," I said in an injured tone.

He hurried off to settle a dispute at one of the card tables, and I went to the rear of the room where Casatelli sat. I was about ten feet from him. He was a tub of fat with $25,000 worth of diamonds on his right hand. He glanced at me with an expression of distaste, tilted his head toward Aldo and said, *"Ques ches?"*

"I don't know," Aldo said. "I never seen the guy before."

"Ask him what he wants," Casatelli said, still in Italian.

Aldo came over and said, "What do you want?"

"I want to see Mr. Casatelli."

Casatelli heard it and said in Italian, "Tell him I'm not here."

Aldo relayed the message to me in English.

I said, "That's a shame," and started to walk away and spun around. "Are you sure he's not here? Are you sure he's not sitting in that chair?" I said, pointing at Casatelli.

A sudden expression of alarm came over Casatelli's face, and he began to get up.

I raised a restraining hand and stepped over to him. "Stay where you are. I'm Dave Toma, and I want to talk to you."

The words carried through the room over the sudden silence, and I could hear chairs being moved.

"All right, Toma, let's go in my office and talk," he said pleasantly. But he knew who I was, and his eyes were uncertain.

"No, we talk right here, in front of everybody." Inside, in his office, he could be his own man. He could say what he wanted to say and offer his own deal without losing face. It can be a big thing for a top mob boss.

I said, "Did you make threatening remarks about me and my family?"

"No. What are you talking about?"

There was a faint sound as Perault started to move toward me. I drew my gun, jammed it against Casatelli's forehead, hard enough to bounce his head back and then slid it down against his face and pointed at his mouth. I shook my head. "Perault arranged to have me tailed, and I don't like that. You understand me, Freddie? Now listen, you slob. When you threaten me, it's bad, but when you try to get to me through my family, you're committing suicide." I jammed the gun against his mouth and drew blood. "I'll blow your head off in a second." I kept the gun pressed against his mouth and pivoted around and faced an army of thugs. "I want every guy in this room to understand. You don't run the city, and you don't threaten anybody."

I looked at Casatelli. "There will be no more threats against my wife and family and no more filthy telephone calls."

He made no reply. His face remained impassive. I'd humiliated him before his lieutenants and soldiers. But I knew the code, the rules that were set down and observed by mob-sters. It was considered stupid to threaten the enemy. Only a fool showed his hand. Nevertheless, there were exceptions by those who threatened openly. It was tolerated and understood. There were some situations that could be handled in that manner. I'd deliberately omitted any references to threats made against me personally.

A threat directed toward a man's family was inconceivable and considered foolish and the most dangerous threat of all since it was one that would rarely be understood by Casatelli's men. A threat like that struck a little too close to home for comfort. Conceivably it was one that could backfire and come to rest at the doorsteps of their own families. Casatelli under-stood it, and so did every man in the room. Casatelli knew with a shrewd intuition that it was something he couldn't get away with.

I had no illusion that I had removed all sources of retaliation that could be directed against me. Seeking Casatelli out in his own stronghold had to serve the purpose of making him lose face. Threatening and demeaning him publicly could only add fuel to the hatred he already had for me. My threat wasn't going to make him close the book on me. I held the gun and walked out of there. Everyone sat and stood as though frozen.

A day later Kendricks called me into his office again, and from the outset, from the way he glared at me, I knew that he had something heavy on his mind.

He said, "Shut the door, Toma," as soon as I stepped in.

We were both standing. He pointed a finger at me and said, "Are you crazy, Toma?"

"I don't think so," I said.

"Well, I got a telephone call that makes me think you're nuts." Anger popped into his voice. "You're going to have to stop this. I mean you can't keep doing whatever the hell comes into your head."

I said, "Listen, I don't know what you're talking about."

He stared at me for a long time. He fought for control before he spoke. "I got a call, an anonymous call from somebody, and he said that you pointed a gun at a guy's head in the presence of a lot of people and that you threatened to blow his head off."

I asked him who the man was that I had supposedly threatened with a gun.

"Don't get smart with me, Toma. Don't turn it around so you're asking the questions. I'm asking you now, right now, goddammit. Did you put a gun to a man's head and threaten to blow his brains out?"

I said, "I don't understand."

Kendricks' fair complexion had become livid. He slammed a hand down on his desk. "You understand, all right, and you're not going to get away with this. When we finish here, I'm going up to see the director. We'll see what he's got to say about a cop who threatens people with guns."

"Who am I supposed to have threatened?" I said again. "If you want me to answer you, you'll have to tell me who it was."

Kendricks pulled a lot of air into his lungs and exhaled slowly. He said, "You put a gun to Casatelli's head."

"How do you know?" I asked. "Was he the one who called you?"

"You think you're a wise guy, Toma. We'll see who the smart one is when we finish up here. It wasn't him on the phone. I already told you that it was an anonymous call."

"But the caller told you it happened to Casatelli?"

"You're goddamn right he did."

"Sure," I said. "I did it. He needed a gun put to his head."

"Sure," Kendricks mimicked. "I did it. He needed a gun put to his head. Now you answer me. Why?"

"They've been threatening my family. There was an obscene call to my wife; they threatened her and my kids. You know I've been busting his banks."

"How do you know it was Casatelli?"

I said, "I know."

"What the hell kind of an answer is that? I want to know how you know. A bird whisper in your ear? How?"

"I know it was him."

"I think you're crazy. I think you're out of your mind."

I'd heard enough from him. "All right, I busted three of his banks and four drops. What the hell are you, stupid? Who the hell else would be calling me, telling me to lay off? The man in the moon?"

He slammed his hand down on the desk again. "You just called me stupid, and I'm going to bring you up on charges."

"No," I said. "You don't listen to the words. I asked you if you were stupid."

He fought for composure, his jaw muscles knotting. "You're a troublemaker, Toma, but we'll see." And now he spoke softly. "Let me remind you of something else, Toma. You're playing with rough people. You think you're rough, but if they want to put the screws into you, you won't have a chance."

I said, "Lieutenant, if I didn't know that you were a cop, I could almost mistake what you're telling me as a direct threat from Casatelli, only you're delivering it."

"I'll bring that up too when I see Spina." He slammed his hands together. "Now, is there anything else you want to tell me that I can tell Spina?"

"Yeah, there is," I said. I spoke slowly, spacing the words out evenly. "Yeah, tell him that I think you're a fool."

And now Kendricks was smiling with a kind of contained fury. In his mind he already had enough on me to hang me with the department. He pointed. "There's the door, Toma."

I got out of there. When I called in three hours later, there was a message that Police Director Spina wanted to see me in his office at once and that it was important. I had a moment's remorse. I wondered if I'd really taken it too far this time, and yet thinking of the threats to my family pushed that right out of my mind. Considering what had happened, I knew that I would have handled it the same way.

I went to see Spina.

"Do you know why you're here?" he said.

"I can guess. Kendricks spoke to you."

He nodded. "Now you tell me exactly what happened. I want the whole bit about you pulling a gun on Casatelli."

He put his hands behind his head, leaned back in his chair and listened intently while I gave him the details.

When I finished, he said, "You're sure it's Casatelli?"

"As sure as a guy can be." Then I told him about the out-of-town man who had been put on my tail and the description I had gotten from him that fitted Perault. I reminded him that Perault was Casatelli's man.

"I know," Spina said softly. "Kendricks also said you called him stupid."

"No. I just asked him if he was stupid."

"There's a difference?" Spina asked seriously. "He's a lieutenant, and he's your superior. He could bring you up on charges for that."

"It was my family that was being threatened. I didn't think that he reacted the way he should have reacted."

"Did you tell him that he was threatening you on Casatelli's behalf?"

"It might have sounded that way to him. I reminded him that I had busted three of Casatelli's banks and four drops; then he reminded me that I was dealing with rough people."

Spina said, "He's right, Toma. On that score, he's right." He paused. "Now let me tell you what happened." He pointed to the glass that covered his desk. "When he started talking about you, he became so angry he started pounding the desk. I thought he was going to break the glass. He kept telling me that he thought you were crazy and that you needed a psychiatrist." He blew a cloud of smoke. "What have you got now, eight, nine thousand arrests? If that makes you nuts, then just go right on being nuts."

I said, "Thanks for the compliment, Director."

"Let me tell you something, Toma," he said slowly. "A good cop who does a job has to get into a little trouble. He makes waves, and people are afraid that the waves are going to wash over them."

I said, "What would you have done if Casatelli threatened your family?"

He took a long time before he answered. He got up from behind his desk and looked out the window. Then he turned and faced me. In a matter-of-fact tone Domenick Spina said, "You took a gun and put it to Freddie's head when he threatened your family. One gun. Who knows? A man's family is his world. Acting as a man, I might have taken two guns and placed one on each side of his head. Family is family. I'm not faulting you for it. As a police officer I might have handled it differently."

I thought D. A. Spina one hell of a cop. If he thought you were right, he'd back you up. It made him special.

I started to get up and he said, "I want you to go back there, and I want you to make an effort to get along with Kendricks. Everybody in the world has got a boss or foreman or a manager, somebody who's a pain in the ass. So I want you to make an effort. He's got his job to do."

"I don't think it's going to work," I said.

"Why?"

"Because I was planning to ask him if I could work alone. I don't want to work with Nichols. He's my partner now."

He lifted an eyebrow. "Jack Nichols? I know Jack Nichols. Why don't you want to work with him?"

"He's not my kind of cop."

"What does that mean?" Spina asked.

"He doesn't like people. If you don't like people, it follows that people don't like you. It's as simple as that. They won't cooperate with a cop they hate."

"He's a tough, hard cop," Spina said. "He'll never change."

"That's my point. It's just as easy to be nice. In fact, I know it's easier. A cop shows people that he really cares for them, and the department comes out smelling like roses. What's wrong with a cop being a nice guy? There are many on the force like that. Cops care about people."

Spina said, "You can't always have your partner tailor made."

"I operate a certain way. I depend on people. If people know there's a pusher in the neighborhood, they'll go to a cop they consider a friend to get him out of there. Just being with Nichols is enough to turn people away. It has to effect my efficiency, and it will. I'd get more results working alone."

Spina sighed. "I can't make an exception in your case, Toma. Suppose every cop on the force came to me with the same request?"

I said, "I'd rather work alone."

"All right. You tell me why."

I gave it a few moments' thought. "Well, first of all, I like to work alone. I've always been more efficient working by myself. I know I can think better. I can do things I couldn't ordinarily do with a partner. When I use disguises, I'd have to tell my partner, now look, this is what I'm going to use. I have to prepare him for it. When I'm out tailing somebody or trying to infiltrate, I don't have that kind of time. I've got to think instinctively. And if I did use a disguise and he was with me, I'd be thinking about his part in the action. What is he supposed to do? Does he hide somewhere? Is he supposed to be part of my act? Suppose the guy can't carry it off and he blows my cover. Then what? If a suspicious hood sees two guys driving around in a car, he can make them as cops. But one guy driving around in a car by himself can pass as a lot of different people. He can be old, young, healthy, sick. He can be anybody. I can do a lot of things that I can't ordinarily do when I've got a partner. I don't have to explain what I'm doing."

"It can be risky, being on your own like that, Toma."

"Yes and no," I said. "There have been many times when I backed out of situations where I could have been hurt, where I've taken a lot of guff. But I've taken it because I didn't have to explain to a partner why I did. I didn't have to impress him that I was a tough, rough guy and that I had to hit back. I don't believe an undercover guy can afford that pride business. If he's in a bar with a partner and his actions result in a fight because a guy pushed him around, the odds are that the owner won't want either of them back in there again. I believe that you can back out with a little class if you haven't blown your cover and when you know that you've got a shot at the target tomorrow. On a job, being humble can pay off. I don't want to have to impress anybody with how tough I am. It's human nature that you don't want to take any abuse from people. So I'd rather be alone. There are many things I can do by myself that I can't do when I've got a partner. He can inhibit me. If I'm alone, I don't have to explain my actions to anybody else. I do my own thing, and it works for me. I don't have to tell my partner to get in the car, or to get down on the floor in back, or even tell him to put on a disguise."

"But there were times when you've had partners working with you in prostitution and gambling and even narcotics," Spina said. "I've been following your record, and I know more about you than you think."

I said, "I operate more efficiently when I'm alone."

He stood up and walked around his office. "You know, you're beginning to convince people in the department. I hear things. Charley Zizza made a friendly bet that you'd have more arrests than any twelve men in the bureau for the month."

I smiled. "So he won. I got lucky."

Spina said, "You make your own luck. You're a loner, Dave. Let me think about your request."

I stood up and thanked him, and we shook hands. As I was going through the door, he called, "Dave," and I turned and faced him.

Spina looked serious. "You know all those news clippings and photographs of yourself in disguises that have been appearing in the newspapers? A lot of those pictures are being hung up in poolrooms and bars. Nicosia busted a couple of number guys, and they were carrying your photographs. It isn't going to get easier for you."

I left. I recalled an evening when I had fooled Spina with a disguise. A man had been thrown out of a window on Mulberry Street. I'd been in the area looking for a pusher. Disguised as a derelict, I'd wandered into the crowd that encircled the dead man. Spina had driven up and with three policemen dispersed the crowd. When I lingered, he had pointed a finger at me and said, "Hey, you, go on home and sleep it off." I ambled off, and he went back to his car.

After a while I walked over and said, "Are you Police Director Domenick Spina?"

He said, "So?"

"Director, don't you recognize a good detective when you see one?"

He looked tired. He stared at me for a moment, and then he laughed. "You bastard."

The transformation of Dave Toma—once a skinny lad (with his sister-in-law Ann) and later, after his Marine hitch. Now he's in the police force—no one to push around.

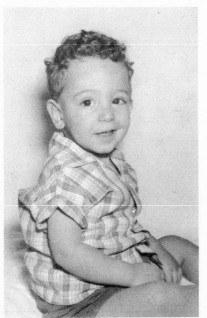

Little David, Jr., who died of asphyxiation in Newark Hospital within forty-five minutes of the time that his father, while on duty, had saved with mouth-to-mouth resuscitation the life of a black youngster who had choked and was apparently lifeless.

Dave and Patricia on their engagement day (with Dave's parents).

Patricia Toma, Dave's wife, getting the children—Jimmy, Janice, Patty Ann, and Donna—off to school.

Dave Toma in some of his typical disguises: a derelict, a priest, a hippie, a prostitute, a doctor, and a hard hat.

Universal-Public Arts Productions

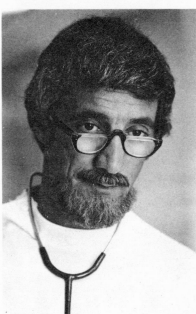

Dave Toma signing autographs for his young admirers on Universal's set.

CHAPTER EIGHT

A neighborhood character named Beanie-the-fast-kid, called to tell me that someone had tried to kill him.

I didn't doubt it. Knowing Beanie and the way he lived, I'd been expecting it for years. "What happened?" I asked.

"I can't talk about it now. I'm in a phone booth down at the piers, and there's guys out looking for me. I got to see you." He gave me the location, and I went to my car and drove toward it.

There's one like him in every neighborhood. He's the one who boasts of his sexual exploits. According to Beanie, he has bedded down every third female in the state of New Jersey, and then when he had used up the supply, he had tried Pennsylvania, New York and Indiana. According to Beanie, his success increased as he went along. I'd known Beanie for years. A bullshitter. As an eighteen-year-old he'd hung around street corners. One night he'd suddenly departed with the whispered comment "I got something waiting for me in Passaic. She's an ex-movie star. What a hump! She just gave me a call that her old man is out bowling and she wants me to come over and take care of her."

Beanie always traveled alone, and most of the guys doubted that he was telling the truth. So one evening five of them followed Beanie and saw him meet an ancient crone on a street corner in Passaic. Some ex-movie star. They drove off and parked on a dark, isolated spot along an embankment of the Passaic River, where they clung to each other for a while. Soon they climbed into the back seat and disappeared from view.

A hurried consultation was held by the viewers, and a number of plans were proposed. Practical jokes can be cruel. The first was to sneak up on the Chevy and turn it over at what they considered an appropriate moment. The second plan was a more ambitious undertaking which involved opening the driver's door, releasing the emergency brake, moving the shift to neutral gear and shoving the car with the fervent hope that it would roll down into the river.

Another strategist had still another plan. He said, "I don't care how busy they are in the back of the car, they'll hear us opening the door and they'll get out of there. What we ought to do is try pushing the car while they're going at it. There's no emergency brake on that clunk, and if it's not in gear, it'll roll. If it doesn't work, then what the hell, we can always turn it over."

There was complete agreement from the others. They waited for a few moments, and when the Chevy began to rock, they advanced and pushed. The slope was about thirty feet long, and the occupants didn't realize they were moving until the car had rolled halfway down.

The ex-movie star screamed. Beanie's startled face appeared at a window. "Jump, jump!" he shouted. Only there wasn't time to jump. They'd run out of time. They were in the river. It could have been serious; luckily the river was shallow. The Chevy sank in mud to its hubcaps. Beanie and the ex-movie star sloshed ashore.

The perpetrators stole off and vowed never to reveal that they had pushed the car into the river. Soon afterward, Beanie-the-fast-kid appeared at the corner with a wild tale. His version was that he'd been out with this beautiful chick and suddenly there were two cars chasing them. There were six guys, and they had fired shots at them. They had managed to escape by driving at high speed over fields. And since he felt that gunmen wanted to kill them he had ditched the car in the river and had saved both their lives. Beanie was not only a liar, he also had imagination.

"Where's the movie star now?" somebody asked. "What happened to her?"

"She took a taxi down to the train station. She said she was never going home again. She was going back to Hollywood. You should have seen the cabdriver when he seen her. He took a look at all that mud, and he didn't want her to get in his cab. Anyway, she said that she'd give him fifty dollars and he told her to jump right in."

Two clunkers and a borrowed truck were driven down to the river. Chain was attached to Beanie's car, and it was towed from its muddy berth. They all helped to get him started.

Beanie had always remained a youth. As he told it over the years, his appeal had become increasingly more devastating to the ladies. They couldn't resist him. Now Beanie was forty years old and still a youth.

It took me fourteen minutes to get over to the piers. He came out from behind a pylon and climbed into the car. I began to make a U-turn, and he said, "Where are we going?"

"If you've got somebody looking for you, then I don't want to sit in one place. What happened?"

"Three guys tried to kill me. They shot at me. No, it wasn't three, it was four."

"Three or four? Which was it?"

"Four, it was four, Listen, I'm scared," he said in a choked voice.

I drove onto the street very carefully, looking in all directions. "Give it to me slow, Beanie."

"There was a guy in a cruddy building who shot at me. He must have fired five shots, two at point-blank range."

"Start again, Beanie, from the beginning. What were you doing there, and who was the guy?"

He threw his arms apart, and I noted that his right hand was cut. "I don't know the guy's name. He was this broad's husband is who he was."

"Nice and slow, Beanie, from the beginning."

"All right, from the beginning. You know Guido Salmone and Harry Helfand? Well, they were hanging around the diner last night and I heard them talking about this broad. I heard them saying that all you had to do was bring a bag of groceries over to her place and you were in. They said she was a great piece of ass."

"So you wanted a piece of the action."

"Yeah, so I ask them who she is and they don't want to tell me. You know Guido, he likes to keep that stuff for himself. And Harry, that wise bastard said that I never give him anything and he wasn't going to tell me. Anyway, we go on like that for about an hour before I soften these guys up. I buy them both dinner, and then Harry says he might as well tell me because Pussycat has got enough to go around for a lot of guys."

"Pussycat?"

"Yeah, that's what they called her. I even asked for her real name, but they said that was it, Pussycat. That was her humping name. When she hears you calling her Pussycat, she'll give it to you right away. They tell me that she's living in a three-story building on Elizabeth Avenue on the top floor. The reason for the groceries is that she's down on her luck and her husband took off with another dame and like that. Now all I got to do when I get there is knock on her door and call Pussycat."

I asked, "Did you ever see her?"

"No."

"How did you get the cut on your hand?"

"By running through the plate glass door downstairs."

I said, "Let's get back to Pussycat."

"I went up there, but first you know that I don't pay for any broad. I don't mind buying the groceries, but you know I don't pay for a broad. There's broads in Pennsylvania, New York and Indiana, hundreds of them, and you know I never paid them for anything. I just give them my line and the next thing they're grabbing at me and—"

"All right, cut the crap. Get back to Pussycat."

"I went out and spent ten dollars on groceries and went over there. The building was dark except for a light on the top floor. I think she was burning a candle. So I knock on the door, and nothing happened. So I knock louder this time, and I'm calling Pussycat, Pussycat. All of a sudden the door flies open and there's a guy standing there in his jockey shorts. This guy looks like a gorilla. He's as big as a gorilla, and he's hairy like a gorilla. He's got a gun in his hand, and he points it at me, and I'm yelling, 'Don't shoot, don't shoot!'

"Then he says that I'm the guy who's been jazzing his Pussycat, and he's going to kill me for that! He fires the gun, three shots. The groceries go up in the air, and he fires again. I say to myself, Beanie, you're dead, and I go flying down the stairs in the darkness with more bullets coming after me. I stumble and fall down half a flight, and when I get downstairs, I run right through the glass door. I jump in my car, and it's got a flat. But I take off anyway because I can see this gorilla run out into the street, and he's firing at me. I go bouncing around the corner riding the flat, and I'm giving it all it can take because I can see a car following me, and it's got guys in there and they're shooting at me. My car is bouncing like crazy on the flat, and the tire rips off, and I'm riding the rim. So I leave it. I jump out. I hopped a couple of fences and went through some backyards and I got away."

"I take it you didn't mention any of this to the police?"

"You take it right. How long do I know you? Twenty-five years? I mentioned it to you."

"All right," I said. "Let's go over to that house on Elizabeth Avenue."

There were shards of broken glass on the front porch. The building was a shambles and deserted. I drew my gun and went up. The door to the apartment was open, and the apartment was deserted. I flashed a searchlight beam over the hall. There were no signs of any bullets that had been fired into plaster or doors.

I went downstairs and got in the car, and Beanie said, "Well?"

"Well? It stinks."

"What do you mean stinks?"

"Stinks means that the guy firing at you was shooting blanks."

"Blanks? Son of a bitch! Blanks," Beanie said. "They set me up. I'm going to get them for that."

"Who are you going to get?"

"Helfand and Salmone."

"Helfand and Salmone. What about the other guys who were chasing you by car?"

"I'll get them,too."

"How many were there?"

"Three, four, maybe five. Who counts when you're being chased and running for your life?"

I dropped him off while he retrieved his car and waited until he changed a wheel. Then I left on a hunch and drove over to Don's restaurant and found Helfand and Salmone drinking coffee.

Harry Helfand and Guido Salmone, two middle-aged jokers. Small-time hustlers and small-time bookmakers and small-time horse players. They were always making big business deals in huddled whispered conferences. They drove Cadillacs and were always a short step ahead of the Shylocks with promises to pay next week.

Guido spoke out of the side of his mouth. "Hey, Dave. What's new?"

I sat down next to them. "What's new is Pussycat and also a guy shooting blanks on top of the stairs at Beanie."

"No kidding?" said Helfand.

"No kidding. You guys are clowns. He could have killed himself falling down the stairs, or he could have had a heart attack, or he could have cut his head off running through a glass door. He could also have killed somebody by running his car on a rim instead of a tire. I don't like it. And he also cut his hand."

"Bad?" asked Helfand in a concerned tone.

"A scratch."

"Who could figure that he'd run right through the door?" said Guido. "He musta crapped in his pants." And now Guido was grinning happily.

"You owe him an apology," I said.

"I'll do better," said Guido. "What does Beanie know about apologies? Nothing. I know a broad in Jersey City. She's a good friend of mine. I'll bring her around one night and give her to Beanie, and she'll tell him that she's Pussycat."

"He'll never believe it."

"He'll believe it because he wants to believe it," said Guido.

I said, "I don't want to hear anything like this blank gun business again."

"Sure," Guido said. "You're the boss. You should have seen him in the hall, don't shoot, don't shoot, he was yelling."

"Who's the guy who fired the blank gun at him?"

Caution glinted in his eyes. "I don't know. Some bum we saw who was walking around. He said he was a wrestler. For ten bucks he was willing to put on an act. I don't know who he is."

I left and went back to my car. It's the ghetto. Sooner or later Helfand and Salmone would devise another form of craziness for Beanie.

I have to admit that I took part in various pieces of nuttiness while on duty. One particular time that comes to mind combined a funny touch with practicality. I was using disguises daily, and I reasoned that if I could deceive the people I worked with, then I would be reasonably safe while infiltrating the world of the criminal. The opportunity presented itself one morning as I was parking on the precinct lot. A painter carrying a bucket of paint and brushes was about to step into the precinct. I broke into a run and intercepted him. He recognized me. "Hey, ain't you that guy Toma, who's been in the newspapers?"

"That's me," I said, and we shook hands.

I asked if he'd do me a favor and go along with a little joke that I had in mind. He listened and nodded as I explained what

I wanted done. I've discovered that most people will go along with a harmless practical joke. He was a mild-looking man. He actually seemed eager to go along with the plan. I borrowed a pair of paint-splattered coveralls from him and put on a wig, beard, mustache and dark glasses. We walked in carrying a twenty-four-foot ladder. I issued orders as the boss painter. We disrupted the precinct. I disguised my voice and shouted, "Drop it, drop it," and the ladder clattered to the floor.

The idea was to see if I could escape detection from the people I'd worked with for years. I walked with one shoulder low and the other high and ran about the squad room wildly, shouting, "Clean off de desks, clean dem off. We going to paint de desks." It was a dialect that I had never heard before.

As if on cue, the painter echoed my words. "De boss wants de desks cleaned off." Suddenly, he was also an actor.

There were piles of paper on the desks of Detectives Artie Calatrella, Joe Burke, and Willie Garcia. I knew they hadn't recognized me when they began to clear their desks. There was also a newly assigned detective. When he had finished clearing his desk, I proceeded to paint it with water. He stared in disbelief, brushed the top of the desk with his fingers, smelled them and said, "Hey, what is this? This is water."

"Of course," I said. "What you want, paint?"

"Are you kidding?"

"Who kids? You want paint, work for de Sanitation Department. Over dere we got paint. We come here, we got no more paint. Dere ain't any paint left for de cops."

Calatrella came over and ran his hand over the desk top. "What the hell is this, water?"

"Of course. I know you don't like de desks painted with water, but dat's de way it is. De boss knows about it, and dey don't want to hear about us being out of paint. Dey tell me dere's no money for paint. You can't fight City Hall. So too bad, we paint with water."

Burke went into Inspector Irving J. Moore's office to report what was going on. The inspector was a different story. He listened while I explained and gestured and ran around the room from desk to desk.

He protested that he had a conference scheduled for today, and in the middle of his protestations, he suddenly threw his head back, roared with laughter and pointed a finger at me. "It has to be Toma," he said.

"Toma? Who is dis Toma?"

And with one gesture Moore ripped my beard off. He revealed that the disguise had fooled him, but it was the improbability of the water act that had tipped him off.

Later that morning. we heard that Paul Perault had been found in the Jersey meadows, with his hands tied behind his back and two bullet holes in his head.

People had been expecting him to get knocked off for years. He'd inflicted lots of pain during his lifetime. Many people wanted to pay him back. It was only conjecture but there were also strong rumors around that Casatelli had known about his wife and Perault and had chosen this time for Perault's execution. Knowing Casatelli, it figured that the cuckold's crown didn't sit too well on his head.

It could have been anybody who knocked him off. It became another unsolved murder.

CHAPTER NINE

The heat was still on to get rid of the prostitutes and to cut down on the muggings. I went back to work reluctantly. I receive no gratification from arresting pathetic and often abused prostitutes. They're victims. Vice squads in major cities pick them up on street corners for loitering with the intent to commit prostitution. They are rounded up and brought in for questioning and fingerprinting. Occasionally they're detained overnight and released on the following morning without complaints being filed against them. It solves nothing. Before the new day has passed, they're back on the street again at a different or even the same location. It's a wishful-thinking method, somewhat along the lines that if you apply enough pressure by harassing her, she'll miraculously disappear from the streets. It doesn't work, and it never worked.

The second method whereby a plainclothesman or detective on the vice squad actually manages to make an arrest after he has been solicited by a prostitute usually results in an arrest that sticks. She does her time. Statistics confirm that when she's released, she'll usually go right back to the "life" again. Incarceration rarely proves to be a deterrent. It's this type of arrest that endangers the arresting officer. He's usually off the street when it occurs, in an apartment, hot-bed hotel room, or a bar. He can be standing on the street near a bar where there is strong likelihood that her pimp or friends can offer opposition to the arrest.

It can be a nerve-racking business for the arresting officer. The apprehension of a prostitute isn't an exact science. I can't say that I normally carry or do not carry a weapon while attempting to apprehend prostitutes. It's what you think the situation will call for that determines that, and yet you're never completely sure that you've taken the right step until after the arrest is made. If she pats you down while you're carrying a weapon and discovers it, she could walk away. But if she panics and calls for help, the game is over, and there's a good chance that somebody will get hurt. Attempting an unarmed arrest can be even more dangerous. There were two experiences involving prostitutes that vividly pointed this out.

There'd been heavy complaints about prostitution and tricks getting ripped off in the vicinity of Howard Street and South Orange Avenue. So at three o'clock on a Wednesday morning I was down there walking about, appearing to be half-stoned. The objective was to be solicited by a prostitute. A vice detective loses his effectiveness after two years because street people recognize him. As a result, it's the usual tour of duty for a vice cop before he's transferred to another department. Disguises have allowed me to remain on the vice, narcotics and gambling squads for twelve years. They allowed me to blend in. The ability to adapt to his surroundings has to be invaluable to any policeman. So I wore a long-haired wig and a heavy mustache. Jack Nichols, my backup man and partner, sat in the car half a block away. I'd left my gun and shield with him. Walking around in the middle of the night in an area as rough as Howard and South Orange Avenue is hazardous. Police are occasionally mugged even though it's rarely reported. The procedure was to remain visible at all times to Nichols. I went as far as the corner, then crossed over to the other side of the street and walked back about twenty feet when she called from a darkened doorway.

"Sssst! Want to have a good time?"

I said, "Sure."

She was a very young, slightly soiled little redhead. She reeked of cheap perfume. "It'll cost you twenty-five," she said.

"You're worth every bit of it," I said.

"Follow me and don't get too close."

I kept what I considered a proper distance. About a hundred feet ahead she turned toward a three-story tenement house. The hallway was lighted, and I accompanied her to the second floor. She then went down a rear stairway to the first floor again. Safety precautions. I thought of Nichols. He had to be told where I was, the building and the apartment number. I was the decoy, and he would be the arresting officer. As she fumbled for her keys, I said, "You know my car's parked about two blocks from here. I wouldn't want it to be stolen. I'll take a walk down and move it closer."

"You leave it right where it is," she said. "The streets are loaded with cops. If they see you parking in front of my place and coming in here, they might follow you."

I grinned at her reassuringly. "I want to bring a little more money back here." Money was what she wanted, but I saw her begin to wonder if she had picked a guy that was going to give her trouble. The business caters to a large variety of men. Tricks can take too long, try to avoid paying and can be creeps or even frightened at the thought of making love to a prostitute.

"You're the prettiest thing I've seen in years," I said. "The trouble is I just brought enough for one time around. I thought that maybe we could go for a doubleheader."

She smiled, but the cold glimmer remained in her light-green eyes. "You could go back for the rest of the money after the first time."

"That would mean I'd have to get dressed again. I get the feeling that I'd like to make it an all-night thing." I glanced at my watch. "It's late. It doesn't figure that you're going to be out much later anyway."

"It'll cost you fifty for a doubleheader." She smiled. "And no matter what happens, I get the fifty. Guys have got big eyes."

"Don't worry about it," I said. "It'll happen, and then I'm going to spend the night."

She told me her name was Ginger.

I went back to the car and briefed Nichols, then returned to the house. Ginger was waiting in the downstairs hallway for me. "Hi," she said. "I was beginning to think that you weren't going to show."

"You kidding?" I asked.

The apartment was a hopeless little cubicle. Worn linoleum allowed me a glimpse of a grimy floor beneath it. A spotlight with a red bulb illuminated a warped mattress, worn linoleum and a juvenile-patterned wallpaper.

I removed my shirt and glanced at my watch. Ten minutes had gone by since I had left Nichols. He'd be at the door within the next five minutes if his timing was right. I wandered over to a vanity dresser. It was covered with a thin coating of face powder, lipstick, tweezers, eye shadow and a jar of cold cream. I saw my face in the cracked mirror behind the vanity. It reminded me that I was tired.

In the mirror I saw the closet door open an inch. It was barely perceptible, but I had seen it. There wasn't any wind in the room. The door hadn't moved by itself. There was somebody in there.

"How are you doing, Tiger?" Ginger called from behind the bathroom door.

"Okay, almost ready?"

I expected Nichols momentarily. He'd come barging through the door like a truck. That was the kind of guy Nichols was. But the man in the closet—and I was sure it was a man—could be trouble if that happened. It figured that he was armed. The play he and Ginger had worked out could be any number of things. They could wait until I was stripped down and take off with my clothes and money. That was the most likely, or it could be something a little more serious than that.

Stalling seemed to be the best bet. I made a great show of removing my pants and folding them neatly over a chair. I removed my shoes and socks.

Ginger came out of the bathroom wearing bikini panties and a big smile. I saw the needle marks on her thighs.

I stared at her and smiled, as though I'd never seen a nude woman before. "You're really gorgeous," I said, and fought like hell not to glance at the closet door. I had a fright going for me that bordered on paranoia. Nichols was overdue. I needed more time. We sat on the edge of her bed and discussed special tastes and preferences.

"Oh, not that," she said with a grimace. "I don't go that way."

I didn't care which way she went. My thoughts were on the guy in the closet. If he was carrying a gun, it could take one round to finish the job.

I suggested another method, and she said, "What's with you, man? What's wrong with the old-fashioned way?"

I became painfully aware that the foot of the bed faced the closet door.

"If I wanted the old-fashioned way, I wouldn't be here," I said.

"Well, I don't know what you think I am, but what you're talking about is not me." She gave me a forced smile. "Listen, we going to fuck or talk?"

I grinned. Time had run out. I cursed Nichols' ancestry and legitimacy quietly, and aloud I said, "We're going to—we're going—" and fell off the bed onto my back.

My eyes stared at her, and then I went into a series of sharp, gasping sounds, followed by a series of sharp, gargling sounds. My eyes rolled around in their sockets.

"What is it? What's the matter?" the redhead cried.

"Wombanitis," I shouted at the top of my voice. "Get my pills, I've only got two minutes. Call an ambulance. No, get my pills." I made a retching sound.

The closet door was flung open, and a guy with a marked resemblance to an abominable snowman sprang from the closet. He was a big, hairless, bleached-out ape. That was him, an ape with a .45 caliber automatic in his right hand.

"What's with this crazy bastard?" he demanded.

"I don't know. He fell off the bed and started going into a fit." She ran for my jacket and turned the pockets inside out. "I can't find the pills," she cried.

"I'm dying, I'm dying," I shouted. "Call the police, call an ambulance, or I'll die right here. Help me, help me."

I was on my back. I made my body rigid, then arched my back, fell back with a choking sound and let my mouth hang half open with a sizable amount of sputum dribbling over my chin. I lay as though dead.

The hairless one said, "Fuck him, that son of a bitch is going to die right here, and the way he's been yelling some son of a bitch probably called the police. Let's get the hell out of here. I'm going," he said and rushed out of the room and ran toward the upper floor, possibly the roof. She gathered her clothes up and tore out after him.

I grabbed my clothes and shoes and left swiftly. I didn't debate pursuing them, not even for a minute. What was I going to do if I overtook the hairless one? Talk to him? He had the gun.

I bounded down the stairs two at a time and sprinted in my socks toward my car. I tried to suppress my rage for Nichols for not having showed up the way we had planned and failed. I cursed him. I'd never liked the son of a bitch anyway.

I drew laughter as I ran past a clump of prostitutes, pimps and assorted scoundrels gathered on a street corner.

A man shouted, "Hey, man, you breaking the fuckin' world's speed record."

I rarely curse, but that evening was an exception. I cursed him and his friends and even his enemies, anybody who knew him. And I managed a few choice words directed at the fates that had me running around naked in the middle of the night.

There was no sign of the car nor of Jack Nichols. A startled cabdriver took a look at the nude man trying to wave him down and immediately mouthed an obscenity, followed by an obscene finger gesture and kept going. He had his own troubles. He didn't need any crazies riding in his cab. I could understand his attitude. I stepped into a doorway and got dressed and then hailed another taxi and was driven to the precinct. I found Nichols, drinking coffee.

He grinned and said, "Well, what have we got here? Where have you been, Dave?"

I was too irritated to be amused. "Where the hell have you been?" I said.

What he was about to say was preceded by a great big laugh,

which drew peals of knee-slapping laughter from three other detectives. "You're not going to believe this, Toma. So maybe I better not tell you about it, since it's probably going to get you steamed."

That brought more laughter from the rest of them.

"Try me," I said. "I won't get steamed. What happened?"

Nichols laughed a little more and then got down to his story. He said that while he had been waiting in the car, a hooker had solicited him. He knew that I was in a room with another hooker and that he was supposed to back me up, but he thought getting an additional arrest would be a great idea.

"What were you supposed to do, take her along with you? You were supposed to back me up."

"There it is," said Nichols triumphantly. "He's getting steamed, just like I said he would. I'll tell you the way it happened, Toma. I was talking to her, and all of a sudden she got into the car. I knew I was supposed to back you, but that's the way it happened. Anyway, the next thing I knew a car pulled up, a guy and a woman jumped out and climbed into the back seat of our car. The next thing the guy did was stick a knife to my throat, and he tells me to drive out of there."

"Just like that?"

"Yeah, just like that. What could I do? So I drove out of there. I wasn't about to try to make a pinch on that street, not when the whole goddamn place is filled with junkies and pimps and there's a chance I'm going to get my throat cut. I got the car up to fifty going through the side streets,and when we got over to Market where there were streetlights, I slammed the brakes on, pulled my gun and told those bastards they were all under arrest. The guy almost shit. I got him to turn around and cuffed him. The broad who was with him tried to jump out the door, and I gave her a little tap to quiet her down. The other hooker up front just sat there, nice and quiet. Anyway, I just got finished booking the three of them."

"If you're finished with your coffee, I'd like to go back to the room where I was and take a look around."

"Let's go," he said, and stood up. "You never did tell me what happened to you. What really happened?"

We went out to the parking lot, and I climbed into the car and drove off with Nichols beside me. I said, "You didn't back me up. She had a guy waiting with a gun."

"Well, I can't go on allowing this guy Toma to keep making all those arrests. A guy has to start looking out for himself. Pretty soon I'm going to get a press agent and a little publicity myself."

"You've got a great sense of humor, Nichols. You're about as funny as an advanced case of leprosy."

"Take it easy, Toma," he said sharply. "Nobody forced you to go with that whore."

"She had a guy hiding in her room with a gun."

"Nobody forced you to go up there unarmed."

"It was the procedure we agreed upon, in case she patted me down."

"That was your idea," he said slowly. "Not mine. I wouldn't go sticking my neck out like that trying to arrest some whore if my job depended on it. They're no fuckin' good. Your trouble, Toma, is that you treat them like anybody else, and you're going to get your brains handed to you one of these days. I would have locked her up right on the street."

"That wasn't the assignment. We weren't sent out to put the collar on a few whores. It was what's been happening to the tricks, they're getting their stupid heads bashed in because the whores are setting them up. That's what we were sent out for."

"That's what you were sent out for, not me," Nichols said.

"I'm not sticking my neck out for some stupid bastard that wants to get laid. If he gets his head broken, that's his tough luck. He ought to know better."

"But he doesn't know better. The hookers are picking up Johns and servicing them and setting them up for their boyfriends to rob them blind."

"Now listen," Nichols said slowly. "I got no use for these people and they've got no use for me. And that's all right with me. Only I don't want anybody telling me how to handle them. I've been working with junkie whores for years and that's something I know how to do. I don't need any advice from anybody, especially you. You and I don't see eye to eye. We never did."

Ginger's apartment was vacant with the door opened wide. Newark isn't a big city in area. There aren't many all-night restaurants. We drove around for fifteen minutes, and I spotted her as she was about to enter a diner. I brought her down to police headquarters. Nichols left as she was being booked.

She seemed to be in control of her emotions while I questioned her. She admitted that she had been arrested twice for soliciting and had done ninety days in the state's work farm for women.

A uniformed cop led her away to a cell. There was a pot of coffee on and I poured myself a cup. No more than ten minutes passed when the door leading to the detention cells opened and the cop who had led her to her cell came in ashen-faced.

"You won't believe it. She just tried to hang herself." He shook his head in disbelief. "I put her in the cell myself. She's all right though. She's alive."

I said, "You? Where was the matron?"

"She wasn't around. I think she was in the john or something."

"How did she do it?"

"With a stocking. She tied it around one of the crossbars and looped it around her neck."

I went down there and found her in a cell. She sat on the floor, her back against the wall, with her face pressed to her knees, wrenching out racking sobs. There was a policewoman with her who kept saying, "But you didn't have to do anything stupid like that. It won't solve anything. What good would it have done?"

I said, "Let me talk to her alone," and when the matron had gone, I knelt. "Who was the man in the closet?"

She looked at me with sudden defiance. "I told you before, there wasn't any man in the closet."

"I saw him run past me when I was down on the floor. It figured that the two of you had a cheap hustle going. What was your friend supposed to do, come out of his hiding place and hit me over the head, or shoot me, or roll me when you and I were in the sack?"

Her mouth tightened. "Now wait a minute. I told you there wasn't anyone in that room besides us."

"How long have you been using junk?"

"You go to hell. I don't have to say anything to you."

"The guy in the closet, is he the one who gets it for you?"

She slid her hand down to her thigh. "This is what gets it for me."

"Where the hell do you get your self-assurance? A minute ago you were trying to hang yourself, and with your next breath you're trying to protect some creep who hides out in a closet."

"There's one thing I know. A rap for prostitution just carries so much time with it. Now what you're trying to get me to say is that there was a guy hiding in a closet while you were in my room. Well, that's a different story, and a judge isn't going to like that. That could get me a lot more time."

"Why did you try to kill yourself?"

"Listen, if I want to talk to a shrink, I'll talk to him. I don't have to say anything to a cop."

"Did you ever try it before?"

"You don't give up, do you? Yeah, I tried it before, twice. Gas and sleeping pills. Somebody always managed to find me before it was all over."

"Lucky. It has to be pretty bad before you try to kill yourself."

"It was. I was feeling low. The second time I tried it I found out that I was diseased. I figured that what the hell, screwing for the world was a slow form of self-destruction anyway, so why not help it along? I tried a bottle of barbiturates." She lifted a hand and touched her throat. "I know that I'm going to be sent away. I don't like the idea of going cold turkey. That's enough to scare hell out of me. I've been through it before."

"It doesn't have to be like that. There are programs that can help you kick it. I can arrange that for you, no problem. We'll taper you off."

"I've been on them before. No thanks."

"What about the guy who was in the closet? I saw him."

She shrugged. "What the hell difference does it make? You're probably going to testify that you saw him anyway. But you're not going to get his name from me. That's for sure. Let me tell you about him. He was the guy who found me after I took the sleeping pills. He saved my life."

"And maybe he's the guy who got you started on horse."

"Smartass, you think you know all the answers." She stared defiantly. "What the hell do you know? I picked two guys up in the street. I took them back to my apartment, and they both went at me at the same time. When they left, I felt like some damn dog crap in the street. I tried to kill myself, that's how low and worthless they made me feel. The guy you saw in the closet stopped me. He gave me my first fix, and I forgot all about how worthless I felt."

"That didn't solve anything."

"Don't try preaching to me. That's the way I live, and I like it. When I'm high, I'm as good as anybody."

I said, "You are. You just have to get your thinking straightened out." I stood up. "I'll see you in the morning."

I went out, climbed into my car and headed for home, and the memory of the tiny prostitute huddled in a fetal position on the floor of her cell remained with me. What did the fetal position have to do with it? Walk into any mental institution, and you can see the patients that way. Was it a wish to remain as a child, or did that posture make smaller targets of themselves?

I don't believe in legalized prostitution. I don't believe a civilized socitey cand subject its members to the destructiveness and degradation of prostitutes. Punishing the prostitutes and the pimps who live off her earnings hasn't really worked either.

Prostitution is a sickness, and you don't treat a sickness in a prison. Prostitution has to be treated by psychotherapy in hospitals and in self-help groups. Instilling a sense of worth and belonging is a goal. It's expensive but no more expensive than the cost of imprisonment. Programs for training in some occupation and a general education have to be of help. Make her more socially useful, and you've got a better person. Prayer won't do it alone. Not even God will help those who don't want to be helped. They've got to want it themselves. Taking a good hard look at the drug subculture from which prostitutes emerge would also help. Going back into the same life situation makes recidivism a certainty.

Reestablishing the value of a human being has to be on top of the list. People have to care about other people; otherwise, the world is a place of hatred. So you try to help the prostitute. She's sick. Punish her for being sick, and it's like punishing people for having ulcers.

I drove south on the Turnpike and couldn't push her from my mind. She'd tried to kill herself. The nagging thought persisted that one day she'd succeed. I was sickened at the waste of all those who were being murdered.

People have to be valued. People need dignity. You just can't let people waste away and die. When we stop caring and loving, we become less than human. I don't believe a woman becomes a prostitute because she wants to be a prostitute. She is what she is because she's mentally sick. She has to be, to subject herself to the punishment that's handed out to her.

During my years on the vice squad I've seen and listened to thousands of prostitutes. I believe they are basically suicidal in that their life is self-destructive. It's a slow death. Some of them had tried to take their lives as many as ten times before they'd gone to sleep for good. Prostitutes know what I'm talking about. There are very few of them who don't know other prostitutes who've attempted to commit suicide. By nature they hate themselves, they feel low, and there is a need to feel degraded and punished. In most cases it's why they become prostitutes in the first place.

There are very few prostitutes who actually enjoy sex. On the contrary, most of them have lesbian tendencies and have homosexual relationships, and in most cases they are active man-haters.

In the cases when they had pimps the theory that they had

selected a pimp because of his sexual prowess was absolute nonsense. It is a bearded myth. It's locker room talk that a whore is a nymphomaniac and has a pimp because she can't find any of her clients who can satisfy her. If she finds a small measure of sexual gratification with her pimp, it is due mainly to the fact that she at least likes him and finds comfort with him.

Prostitutes are among the loneliest people in the world. The pimp, by just being there and by being somebody she can go home to and speak to, provides her with company. He provides a measure of peace of mind.

He is the man who would raise bail when she is busted. Most of the prostitutes I knew felt that their pimps were their protectors. He was somebody who would look out for her when she is sick. Nobody is going to rip her off while her man is around. Prostitutes are often assaulted by their clients and held up and robbed during the night hours. In many cases they form an attachment to pimps for the reason that he is a hard character who wouldn't allow that to occur. Often his reputation would be enough to allow her to work unmolested. He would protect her from exploitation by anyone except himself.

I've known pimps who were also con men, thieves, confidence men, hustlers, small-time bookmakers, drug addicts, pushers. There were even vice squad detectives who had become pimps and had been arrested for it. Newark isn't any different from any other large city with a vice problem. Occasionally detectives shook prostitutes down and were apprehended for it. They had affairs with prostitutes. Police are human like everybody else. I knew vice plainclothesmen who had arrested prostitutes and eventually married them. In a few cases the marriages had worked out fine, but in most cases they failed. It wasn't just the infrequent vice cop. I knew some highly respected businessmen who had also taken that path.

Violence between prostitute and pimp was a fearsome thing. Her jealousy of the other girls in his stable often triggered arguments that ended with knifings, ice pick attacks, beatings, bullets and murder. She attempted to ingratiate herself on the one hand and denigrated him on the other by referring to him with contempt as her "pimp." She rationalized that if she gave him money that she earned in a base manner, somehow the money was tainted, and his acceptance of it made him lower than herself.

In many cases it was the girl's promiscuity often caused by fears of homosexuality that led her into the life of a prostitute. She sought friends who were like herself. Friendships were formed with prostitutes, drug addicts and criminals. Eventually it was suggested to her that she could be making money for what she was giving away gratis. It wasn't always the complete reason for her choice of prostitution, but it was for many prostitutes I've known.

I would oversimplify if I stated that there are specific reasons for the choice of prostitution as a way of life. It's a complex problem. People throw their hands up in the air, as if to say, "What can we do about it?"

Nobody knows all the answers. I do believe that some of the answer lies with the family. It has to stand for love, affection and self-worth for its members. The family has to be home and refuge and a place for genuine relationships. It has to be a place of love.

If it's a place of love, it can withstand the outside pressure of those who would tear its members apart. In my father's garden the tomato plants flourished because of tender loving care. They didn't grow strong by themselves. The young woman who has a good family relationship and who knows love and kindness there does not become a prostitute.

It's a sleazy business that concerns itself with low morality and exploitation. The exploiters are the dregs at the bottom of the barrel. If I had to name the lowest form of humanity, it would be the pimp who deliberately turns a girl on to drugs. He's rotten. Shoplifting, stealing, breaking and entering, rolling drunks and prostitution have to become her way of life. To think otherwise is naïve. He's an animal who deliberately destroys her for self-gain.

There were times when I've arrested as many as fifty prostitutes a month. Most of them involved the prostitute when she was with her client. It didn't always work out that way, but it was a situation that I preferred, rather than go in myself as the prospective trick with the possibility of an entrapment defense that could get easy dismissal.

Living within the world of prostitution as a vice detective, I've heard and observed bizarre things that defy the imagination. Many of the girls, even after I had arrested them, became friendly. They often spoke to me. Talking to them, trying to convince them to get out of the "life" rarely worked. But there were times when I can honestly say that I've convinced prostitutes to turn a new leaf and attempt to live differently. One opened a tiny grocery store, little more than a stand. She made it work. Another did it with a salesgirl's job. There were others. The one fact that I observed about those who managed to break away was that they did it elsewhere. Usually they moved to another town where they weren't known and began a fresh start. Motivation came in strange ways. A girlfriend who'd been tortured or murdered raised fears for them. But they seldom moved if they were drug-addicted. Leaving an area where they had a connection to make a score was inconceivable. They were trapped.

A man on the prowl for a prostitute in the middle of the night in a dangerous crime-filled area isn't thinking properly. Often he is the prey of the prostitute and her confederate. She'll pick him up, and then as they start to go to her place, she'll warn him that they are in a bad area and say, "I hope you've got enough sense not to be carrying more money than you really need for me." Then she suggests that he leave his wristwatch, money, keys, personal identification and credit cards in his car under lock and key. She doesn't try to make him too apprehensive. She mentions that it's never happened to any of her customers, but she has heard of people being held up on the street.

He believes her because the idea of bedding her down is predominant in his pants. She walks back to the car with him while he stashes his valuables and locks the car as her hidden confederate observes the car's location. They then go to her place where she prolongs the action. Instead of the customary hurry-up job, the trick can't get over his good fortune at really finding a girl who is unhurried and who seems to be genuinely fond of him.

When he returns to his car, he finds that it has been broken into, or in many cases stolen, because he left his keys. His money, personal property and credit cards are gone. If he thinks of what might have happened, he can consider himself fortunate. I can remember others who'd had their clothes ripped off by someone working with the prostitutes and had been badly beaten. Stripping the clothes from tricks and then stealing their valuables were a favorite method used to discourage pursuit. I'd also seen them after they were tossed from buildings and through windows.

Once I'd been assigned to a special prostitution detail that was trying to bust a ring that catered to groups watching a staged performance of girls being taken against their will.

The viewers were supposedly intelligent men, but it was

amazing to see how many of them actually believed that they were going to see what was forcible rape. It took place in a first-rate motel. There were twelve viewers, including myself. From peepholes in an adjoining room we watched what had to be the worst piece of acting I had ever witnessed. The opening scene began with a couple entering the room and the girl pretending apprehension. She'd never gone to a motel room with a man, she said, and she reminded him of his promise that there would only be some light fooling around and nothing serious. She was immediately reassured by her companion that it was all he had on his mind. He fed her a few drinks, and they both went into their act. He was the oversexed brutal male, and she was the terrified virgin fighting for her honor. She fought desperately, running around the room. Finally he forced her to accede. At first she was completely unresponsive to him, and then it became obvious, despite her firm resolution, distaste and abhorrence that she became a victim of her own passions. It was the accepted format for a hot book. A little bit of male chauvinism, the thought being that a woman really enjoyed rape. Ask a woman who's had her teeth knocked out or who was terrified for her life, and you'll hear it the way it really was. Some of the viewers detected the sham and left shame-faced and sad. Others detected it, forced the thought from their minds and viewed the performance as somehow being genuine. A man and a woman became genuinely aroused. In the audience of twelve there were two women. Another saw great mirth in it and had to be cautioned from laughing out loud by the pander, who didn't want our presence made known. I left partway through the show, made a phone call and had the assistance of twenty policemen to arrest everybody, including the motel's management.

There were also voyeurs who would pay for a performance

by two girls and would then have relations with one of the girls, or they could be hiding watching a performance by a man and woman.

I can remember prostitutes telling me that they had Johns who were only sexually potent with them. Others went to prostitutes for the sexual variety that they could not find with their own wives.

There were tricks who insisted that the girl use obscene language during intercourse. For the prostitute there was also the violent world of sadism and masochism. I saw prostitutes who had been severely whipped and clients who found it necessary to have themselves beaten before they could engage in any sexual activity. Prostitutes wearing short leather garments and hip-high leather boots were some of the ones who catered to their requests.

There were also tricks who could enjoy sex after they had degraded and defiled the girl in ways that I won't discuss. When she was degraded in these bizarre performances, it had to make her feel completely worthless.

But who was going to change the nature of a man looking for a woman? Restlessness, loneliness, boredom, a wish for tenderness and love—I'd heard all of that from Johns. One of them said, "With my wife it's maybe twice a month, and it's like she's doing me a big favor. She makes it her business to let me know that she doesn't enjoy it." There was an old man who told me that his wife had died and that women didn't want anything to do with him. "I'm grateful that there's a prostitute around when I want a woman," he said. Nobody knows all the answers. I do know that I'm not the one who can sit back in judgment on people.

Sin and salvation are not my game. But what are you supposed to do when a prostitute with a broken jaw tells you that she has a two-hundred-dollar a night quota to meet and that her pimp has beaten her black and blue and broken her jaw because she didn't meet her quota? God help her. A beast of burden would fare better on this earth.

You can pay for steak without getting steak for your money. I arrested a prostitute and her John and brought them down to headquarters. I learned that he was married, and I recall saying, "You know a lot of these hookers have venereal disease. Didn't you think of that?"

He appeared crestfallen but only for a moment. "I know," he said. "She was really something," I never had a woman who could move like her. She got her legs up and around my back, and she really moved that thing, up, down, back and forth, side to side and then in a cricle, grinding it away." He spoke in an awed tone.

A policewoman came up from the detention cells and signaled me to come over. "Everything happens to you, Toma," she said, smirking.

"What?"

"You won't believe this."

"What? What happened?"

"That woman you brought in. We searched her. She isn't a woman."

"Oh? She's not a woman? Maybe she's a giraffe?"

"She's a man."

I said, "Ah, Marrone!" I went back and resumed conversation with the John. "She really must have been something."

He smiled. "I'll never forget her. I never had action like that. Up, down, back and forth, sideways and in a circle."

"Well, you're going to remember her a long time. I have news for you. She's a guy."

"A guy!" he cried in tones of disbelief. "I'll be a son of a bitch. It was dark, I couldn't see," he explained. "A guy. What am I going to do?"

"Nothing. For you it could have been a hunk of liver." I advised him to carry a flashlight in the future.

CHAPTER TEN

Driving in the following morning, I thought of Nichols and his hatred for people, and I knew that there was nothing I could say to him that was going to change his attitude. I remember him years ago when he was a radio patrol cop, saying, "Mollycoddling these people isn't the way to control them. Do a little head whipping. Give the policeman the power that was once his, throw some of those people in jail where they belong, and you'd soon see how all this lawlessness will stop."

Beating people wasn't the answer then. It never was. And I say it now, during a time when the average cop working a ghetto district worries about whether or not he will return home from his tour of duty.

A sniper fires at a policeman he doesn't even know because he's been told the policeman represents authority. And yet the man he wounds or kills is the one who will rush into a burning building to save the sniper or his family if need be. The climate in the ghetto toward the police and the pressure in the department toward its own members are different today. The commander of a precinct where poverty is pervasive and life is hazardous is aware of the dangers facing his men now more than ever. Caution, tact, understanding and sensitivity for the area's residents are the guidelines that have to be observed. The ghetto is one big time bomb.

It's hard to understand blacks giving a black or white cop who's trying to break up a fight between blacks a hard time. And it's even more difficult to understand why a slum kid would stone a fireman who is attempting to extinguish a fire in his own neighborhood.

And the disturbing thought comes through that maybe the black or the poor white and the Spanish-speaking kid has so little to look forward to that he really doesn't give a damn whether his neighborhood burns down or not. Blacks don't see the police officer as a nice man who helps little children cross the street and returns them to their parents when they're lost.

Because of inadequate opportunities, young slum dwellers are constantly hustling. Hustling—that is, the business of making money on the side or in a shady, illegal manner—is not the exclusive provence of the slum dweller. A hustler's sphere can encompass that minute number of police who operate outside the law. Police are human, and they've got their weaknesses as well as their strengths; but by and large policemen protect life and property, arrest and detect offenders and prevent crime. They try to perform that duty in the neighborhood where they are assigned.

The cop has a job to do, and he does it. When he works in a poor-white, black or Puerto Rican area, he's there to protect the people and to look out for their rights. The majority of the people in the slums know it, and they depend on him. They want a mugger apprehended in their own neighborhood the same way the middle class or the affluent want it in their own.

People have to have hope. Take hope away from people, and all that remains are resignation and self-hatred. I can remember arriving upon a crowd of hundreds of people viewing a scene of two men outside a bar in the Central Ward, slashing at each other's faces with razors. Blood stained the sidewalk red. When I tried to get through to break up the fight, I heard the threats: "Mind your own business. Man, stay out of it, or you'll never walk out of here."

The fight ended with both men streaming blood and walking off in different directions. I'll remember the incident as long as I live. Drug addicts and ghetto people have a low opinion of themselves. They're not as concerned with their health and their bodies as the more affluent. It accounts for the apathetic response of the participants and spectators toward the razor slashing scene.

People without hope don't care about themselves, and this little thought has its own special kind of horror accompanying the illness. The addict says that he uses heroin because it makes him feel alive and being alive is meaningful and not a foolish waste. Show him some understanding, say the psychologists, and he'll stop using heroin. It's an oversimplification and a sugar-coated pill. Life doesn't become meaningful to the addict, merely tolerable. Euphoria is a temporary state. He can sit in a group and he's alone, stoned, lost, staring into space. He's a zombie, and nothing matters to him. What's meaningful about that?

Understanding the problem and what causes it can be just so effective. A more effective method says that you don't have heroin addicts when there is no heroin to be purchased.

The mugging victim who's been clubbed, stabbed and

robbed of $8 by a junkie has an altogether different opinion of what should be done with the addict. Death by hanging, electrocution, beheading and life imprisonment are a few of the victim's suggestions for his assailants.

Detective Jack Nichols had his own solution for narcotics addicts, whom he hated with a fanaticism bordering on insanity. "I'd cut their balls off," said Nichols. "Yes, sir. I'd castrate them." However, if there was one thing to be said for Jack, it was that he was democratic in his hatred for addicts of different coloration.

Nichols was a tough cop and might even have been called a good cop, except for the fact that he was bigoted, and the burden of having to hide his emotions from the blacks seriously impaired his efficiency in dealing with them. It made him a bad cop. The blacks, reacting with a built-in radar system, finely honed by their years of dealing with all types of bigotry, called Nichols a fuckin' white pig. As far as he was concerned, they were all indolent free loaders who were living off the taxes that he paid. He was a massive man. He was built like an ox, and he thought like an ox, and he thought nothing of skull knocking kids just to keep them in line.

He was a throwback to the not so distant past when the Central Ward had been a dumping ground for the department's undesirables, such as on-the-take cops, drunks and sadists and others of that ilk who had formed and molded the ghetto dwellers' image of the cops over the years.

Needless to say, Newark's citizens and Detective Jack Nichols had unfavorable impressions of each other. It was not totally unexpected when Nichols, in response to a call, narrowly escaped having his brains splattered all over the sidewalk by a garbage can that was dropped from the roof of a tenement by a youngster who had once had his skull bashed by Nichols.

Whereupon Nichols had drawn his service revolver and had fired six shots in the general direction of the bombardier, a blasting which resulted in three shattered front windows, lights being doused in the immediate area and numerous complaints from civil rights organizations on the following morning, most of which were ignored, because Nichols denied firing any shots. He hated people. I'm not singling out Nichols as a cop who hated people. I believe he would have hated people if he had been a plumber, shoemaker or scientist. There are people like that. I know that I couldn't work with him as my partner. It came to a head when we learned that Eddie Johnson had been released from the penitentiary and was back on the street. Nichols had busted him, but I had known Eddie Johnson first.

I met him during a bitter snowstorm five years ago. I was doing surveillance on a shoot-up pad. I'd gone into the building and established that the vacant apartment held drugs. At two on Sunday morning I'd stationed myself in a narrow walk between two buildings across the street which gave me a view of the building. I was waiting for the pusher and the addicts to show. A little light filtered down from a window and revealed a sleeping wino huddled in the snow with his head resting on a garbage can cover. Somebody had given him a gash across the bridge of his nose. I let him sleep.

At the mouth of the walk the figures of three men stealthily appeared, entered the alley and took up positions pressed back against the walls. They seemed to be watching the shoot-up pad across the street. They could have been addicts waiting for the connection or possibly waiting to rip him off. It was a daily occurrence for junkies to take off pushers and addicts for drugs or money.

A few minutes went by, and I heard a whisper from the figure on the right. A young man began to pass the alley's entrance, and the three men sprang. The one on the right got his arm around the youth's neck. Another assailant helped drag him into the alley. It wasn't an easy battle. The victim struggled. I could hear the sound of fists hitting flesh and cursing and then there was a metallic glint, and a knife held by an attacker drove downward toward the youth. He fell on the snow-covered ground and tried kicking at his attackers. It all happened very quickly. One of the men punched downward. The two others kicked him savagely.

I drew my revolver and charged toward them, yelling, "Hold it! Police!" They scattered like buckshot. When I got to the street, there were two men running off to the left and the other to the right. He seemed to be the slowest of the three. I turned and broke into a run.

It wasn't his night to be overtaken.

Behind me, the mugged youth called, "Help me, help me."

I went back and played my flashlight over him. Blood burbled in his nostrils. He'd been stabbed in the chest, and the snow on which he lay was red slush. He couldn't have been more than fifteen. At the rate he was losing blood no ambulance would ever reach him in time.

I knelt beside him. He looked at me. "They kicked me, mister. They kicked my face and I'm stabbed bad. I don't want to die. I'm going to die in this alley, man."

I said, "Don't talk," and got behind him and grasped him under both arms and dragged him down the block, trailing blood to my car.

I let go of him to open the passenger door, and his head thudded on the sidewalk. He made no outcry. He was as still as the falling snow.

A window opened in an upstairs apartment, and a woman shouted, "What are you doing with that boy? I'm going to call the police." And then she was screaming, "Police! Police!"

I lifted him, his head bouncing on my chest and got him onto the front seat. I heard blood gurgling in his chest. I hit the brights and the siren button and tore out of there, aiming the car toward the nearest hospital. The late hour of the night was in his favor; the streets were deserted of traffic. I glanced at the spreading pool of blood and reached over and shook him to reassure myself. He made a small sighing sound, and his head slumped forward.

The emergency room at the hospital was a scene of bedlam. Newark on a Sunday morning at two twenty. It was as though a bomb had exploded, and the victims were all gathered together. I saw gashed throats, gunshot wounds and a stomach knifing. The floor was slippery with blood.

An intern looked at what I was carrying and said to a nurse, "Get his blood type, and get his blood down here fast!"

I laid him out on an emergency table. Within minutes there was a bottle of blood hanging over him, draining into his arms.

When you save them, they belong to you. Once he shuddered convulsively, and I called the intern, and he opened his eyelids and took his pulse. The intern smiled. "He just went to sleep. I think he'll be all right."

I looked around. The emergency room had finally emptied. They brought him upstairs to the ward, and I went home. I visited him on the following day and learned his name, Eddie Johnson. He had been working in an office building cleaning up and was on his way home when the attack took place. He smiled at me. "Man, you saved my life. Those cats really wanted to do a job on me when I started to fight."

I said, "Did they get any money from you?"

He flashed a triumphant smile. "I had five dollars, and I still got it. I wasn't about to let them take it from me."

"There were three of them," I said. "They could have killed you."

"Yeah, I know that now," he said thoughtfully. "But I'd been working for that money. I was just too mad to be frightened. I got frightened later when I woke up in this place."

That was five years ago. Nichols busted him two years later for car theft. It was his first offense. He was sentenced to five years and did two. Then he was back, and we heard that he was selling heroin and pills. I went looking for him before Nichols could find him and bust him. I found him first. I tried to tell him what it meant and where he had to wind up. I explained that I lived with it, and I had worked with addicts on the street and in rehabilitation centers all over the state.

He wasn't the same kid I'd pulled out of the alley. "Yeah, I know about what you've been telling me. But how come if you know so much about it that your own nephews are hooked?" It was an argument I'd heard many times before from other addicts trying to rationalize their existence.

"I tried to help them, but I couldn't control them, not everybody listens."

Eddie Johnson couldn't quite believe it when he saw me take the cuffs out of my back pocket.

"Come on, man, you're not going to run me in. Hell, you're the guy who saved my life. Remember? Come on, give me a break."

I said, "How did you get started, Eddie?"

"What are you doing, Dave? I already told that to a shrink."

"Tell me."

He shrugged. "You know."

"I don't know."

"You know, the way a lot of guys get started. I smoked a little pot, and then tried a little hash."

"I know. But you're on scag now, and you're peddling it, to keep yourself together."

"Funny," he said. "I didn't get right on that. I couldn't get

myself to start jabbing that needle into my vein. I could skin
pop, but that was as far as I'd go."

"You're hooked, Eddie. You've got a problem."

"Blame that on speed. I got into that scene, and I got over my
fear of the needle."

I said, "Eddie, you knew better."

He stared at me. "You know better too, Toma."

"I don't understand you, Eddie."

"I guess it's all in getting used to knowing that you're
nothing. I keep thinking of all that bullshit whitey's been
handing out to me as long as I can remember. Go to school, and
you'll get a good job, and things are just going to be great for
you. That's all crap. Take a look at what you see on television,
how all those people are living real cool. You've been in the
slums of Newark. Where do you see that kind of living?"

"That's advertising, Eddie. Somebody's trying to sell
something to a viewing audience. It's nice to look at a nice
apartment. It puts people in a better frame of mind so they can
be more easily influenced by the commerical that comes next.
Not everybody lives that way."

"Listen, Toma, don't try to con me. I know who I am. It's me
you're talking to, Eddie Johnson. I was dead from the minute I
was born. That's me, poor black son of a bitch, born into the
welfare system, old man unknown and your mother a domestic
and can't take care of you. So you look around and you see
whitey making it with his education and good jobs and clothes,
and you know there ain't no use of your trying, because there
ain't nobody who's going to hire you, even if you do know
anything, because you're black. And so you say, 'fuck whitey,'
he ain't any good and he's never going to be any good, because
he really doesn't give a good goddamn whether you live or die.
He hates you. Hell, he don't even want to know that you exist.

He'd just as soon forget about you. When I was sixteen, I stole a car one night just to take a ride the hell out of that shithole I was living in. It must have been a hundred and twenty that night, that's how hot it was, people hanging around on the street all night because if they stayed inside those shacks they would be roasted. I got stopped, and they took me in, and they brought me up before a judge, and he made me a ward of the juvenile court. Juvenile court my ass—criminal courts is what they are and a conviction will mark you for life, as though just being black isn't enough."

So Eddie Johnson was tried and convicted and sent away. He did his time. A week after he was released he was found dead in a shoot-up pad in the North Ward. The heroin contained strychnine.

So you say a prayer, God have mercy on Eddie Johnson—and yourself too, because you can't forget all the Eddie Johnsons you've known.

I couldn't forget what he had said about my failure to help my addicted nephews. Perhaps a touch of guilt remained for me. A week earlier my nephew Ronnie in a narcotic stupor, with veins collapsed and pus-filled needle holes on both arms, had seen me driving along Market Street. He ran toward the moving car and with outstretched arms had thrown himself on the hood. He begged me to run him over and put him out of his misery. He was so far gone at the time that he was using anything he could get his hands on, morphine, heroin, cocaine, black-market methadone and barbiturates. For twenty-three years he'd been walking the streets with the junkie nods, battered and beaten and sniffling. There were times when he had completely freaked out and gone out of his head as a result of the wrong mixture of drugs and alcohol. I'd locked him up no less than twenty-five times, and no matter what treatment he was given he grew progressively worse. I'd seen him scratching, stinking of filth, vomit and excrement, not caring whether he lived or died. I'd seen my sister and brother-in-law shed tears, pray, hospitalize him, bail him out of jail, commit him to mental institutions and enroll him in every drug rehabilitation center in the state. They'd even locked their door against him but had always relented and taken him in again. Once I'd received a call that he was hanging over a fire hydrant on South Orange Avenue. I brought him back to the Fourteenth Precinct, where I was assigned, and cuffed him to the wrought-iron fence outside. I recall that I couldn't bring myself to carry my nephew inside, draped over my shoulder like a side of beef. What can you do when everything had been tried without success? He was lost. He didn't know who he was or that he existed as a human being. I went in to see Lieutenant Dougherty and broke down when I began to tell him about Ronnie chained to the fence like a dog.

Dougherty went out there with me, and we carried him in and placed him in a cell. Dougherty locked the door and placed the key in his pocket. "Let him sleep it off. We'll keep him in there until he gets it out of his system."

Ronnie begged me to get him out when I visited him on the following day. I refused. I doubted that Dougherty would have given me the key to the cell then, even if I had asked him for it. On the third day Dougherty contacted me by radio to come in. Withdrawal had begun for Ronnie.

"Let me in there," I said to Dougherty. "I'm going to stay with him." I went in, and he locked the door after me.

From inside the cell I asked Dougherty to call my wife and explain to her that I wasn't coming home until the ordeal was over.

I remained with him for days, while he screamed, shook with

chills, vomited, suffered diarrhea and rolled on the cell floor in pain. He begged for a fix, cursed me, tried to attack me and finally attempted to smash his head on the cell wall.

When it ended, he was so weak that he had difficulty standing up. I delivered him to my sister. Two days later he left and went right back on junk again.

But they are not all destroyed, and I know the statistics. Maybe it sounds naïve, but I believe that most addicts in the country can be cured with rehabilitation programs and, even more important, love and understanding. You don't ever shut the door on them. I refuse to accept negative attitudes toward helping them. I don't care what anybody says about lack of hope for the addict. I know differently. I've seen them come back.

They have to do it themselves, but before they can, they have to know that you have fai in them. They've got to know that there is someone they can call, no matter what hour of the night. Somebody has to be there to listen to them, to sympathize and to help them get through the night. You have to care for people. Getting a call from an addict at three o'clock in the morning, listening to him speak until the sun rises, has been referred to by my wife as Toma's curse. I've had Father George Lutz call it Toma's blessing.

Talk to someone who is in the living hell of drugs, lend a helping hand, give him a kind word and the assurance that he needs to last out his agony, and you're doing God's work. It may sound corny, but there's no other way for me to describe the satisfaction, gratification and the plain down-to-earth feeling of riches that I experience when I see someone who has fought his way back.

Take Johnny Shylo, for instance. That's what he calls himself, Shylo, meaning he was always shy the money for a fix and he was always too low. At this moment he is my personal triumph. Johnny Shylo, age twenty-three, a house painter, has been clean for ten months.

He's never known a father, merely a succession of "uncles." When he was six, he recalls sleeping in the back of the local dogcatcher's truck with his two-and-a-half-year-old sister in the company of four dead dogs. The dogcatcher-uncle, who was recovering from a broken leg, beat the sister because he wanted her to go to the bathroom and smashed Johnny over the head with his crutches because he protested. At nine Johnny Shylo was addicted. At eleven he was thrown out of school.

At thirteen Johnny Shylo lived with a twenty-seven-year-old hooker named Betty, who had a child by him. She had two children of her own and a husband in jail for armed robbery. She told him how good heroin was and drove him to Harlem, where she used her welfare check to buy the first fix for him. Half a load, fifteen bags. Eventually he got to the point where he was shooting half a load at a time. He was big for his age and looked older. He held up gas stations while Betty waited for him in her car. He gave her the money for drugs. Holding somebody up with a gun is like being two different people, he has said. "You stand there with a gun in your hand like an animal. You're scared to death while you're pulling a stickup, and anybody who says differently is full of crap," said Johnny. I'd heard it the other way around from stickup men who experienced a sense of complete power while watching their victims begging for their lives and actually gagging with fear. That sense of power can only be called a sickness of the mind. At fourteen Johnny Shylo was apprehended while sticking up a gas station, and one of the arresting officers knocked two teeth out of his mouth.

He went to jail and was released three years later. At nineteen he was in Kearny trying to cop some dope when he saw two detectives across the street. He immediately swallowed two tablets of LSD that he had in a pocket. He went home and drank a glass of water and saw a drop spread six feet wide. In his darkened bedroom the taillights of a passing car cast a red illumination over the room. He saw a man who was nine feet tall in a purple robe, with the horns of the devil protruding from his head. The giant swung a dead dog like a pendulum. So Johnny Shylo ran to the kitchen drawer, grabbed a knife, and stabbed the walls and the headboard of the bed and ran screaming into the street. The episode earned him a stay at a mental hospital where he recognized no one for three months.

And from this he came back to being a functioning human being. I got him into D.A.R.E., a drug rehabilitation center, where Johnny broke his habit. He tells me that I saved his life by getting him off drugs. He tells me that there is no way he can lie to me, that I really care.

Drug addicts and former drug addicts have told me they have faith in me. How can I not have faith in them? I do. I have faith in them. I've seen hundreds who have made it back. I've seen them as low as Johnny Shylo, like mindless vegetables, and they've made it back.

When you've seen them at the bottom, when people become less than human beings, it can cut your patience short with those who make light of the drug scene. I've seen comedians capitalize on drug skits, mimicking stoned addicts, and I've heard audiences laughing uproariously. Years ago comedians worked a similar routine by exploiting the alcoholic. He too was a funny man; indeed, he was about as funny as a human being who was dying of cancer, diabetes, heart trouble and a host of other cute, funny little sicknesses.

I've got even less patience with college professors and civil libertarians who advance theories that depriving people of drugs will somehow infringe upon their rights and freedoms. Freedom from what? The right to reduce a human being to nothing? The right to bring innocents into burglary, murder, prostitution, violence and the complete human degradation of the human spirit? Are these the rights they're fighting for? What about the rights of people who love them? Where are their rights? What about the victims?

I've listened to the young, and there's a heaviness that goes with it. I can't disassociate myself from the young after I've locked them up. I want to know why they stole or assaulted or prostituted themselves. If I know the reason, then perhaps I can talk to them and prevent them from doing it again.

They've called me at all hours of the night to tell me their troubles, and they ask for advice. People have to have someone who will listen to them. I've told them that addiction is physical. It's an escape from reality. It's running away from problems. People have got to stand up and face problems and ugliness. It isn't easy. It was never easy. Occasionally parents have to be able to say no to their children. And saying no is also love. A degree of firmness is love. Letting your youngster run completely on his own, without parental concern or guidance, is the height of foolhardiness. You don't have to overpower your children, but you have to let them know that you care for them. They're accountable, just as you're accountable.

I've seen the young after they've fallen, and I've listened to them saying, "Why didn't they stop me? Look at me now. I'll show them. I'll make them pay for not loving me."

I listened to Johnny Shylo as he shook with sweat pouring from his body, saying, "I can kick it. I got into it, I can get out of it." He's called me up when he feels that he has to shoot up, and I've talked him out of it. For Johnny Shylo there's no yesterday, there's only today. He says, "Today I'm beating it, even if I have to do it minute by minute. Every ten minutes you beat it, you've lived ten minutes." Shylo tells me that he can identify with me. He tells me that I'm for real and that I'm too good to be a cop and that I'm in a bastard line. That doesn't make me special. He'd say the same thing about any cop who'd offer him a helping hand or any other human being for that matter. He says cops and prison guards have to know how to handle people. He weeps as he tells me of the time he was in the Jersey City jail and two addicted youths of seventeen and eighteen were raped the first night they were there. Sixteen inmates held them down and screwed them. Horrors. How long has it been since we swung through the trees?

Shylo is a press agent. I've heard Johnny Shylo say, "Toma knows how to keep you straight. He's not out to lock you up. He talks to you as though he's a junkie himself. He knows exactly how you feel." I do know. I've heard him say, "Hearing about another guy who can't make it back is frightening. I'd rather get shot than go back to it."

I've seen him come back from the depths to function as a human being. These are the moments for me. I came into the world naked, and I'll go out the same way. Money is not my God. But there have been the moments in my life when I've attempted to help people and have seen it work. It is at these times when all the gold and silver in the world can't match my victory. When it happens, I am the richest man in the world.

Victory and defeat are not taken lightly by me. I've seen the Eddie Johnsons who haven't made it back, and they've provided bleak moments of desolation and despair when I've wept like a child.

Recently Johnny Shylo called me on a Friday morning to tell me that he had been stabbed by a passerby while he sat on the front stoop of the building he lived in. He was on his way to Newark Hospital, and he'd lost blood heavily.

At the hospital a nurse told me that there was no record of a Johnny Shylo.

"He was knifed," I said. "I spoke to him earlier, before he left for the hospital, and he said an ambulance had been called, and this was where he was going."

She peered at the list again and said, "I'm sorry, we don't have him." And then she looked again and said, "The only knifing victim that was admitted this evening was a man named John Toma, with a severe knife wound in his chest."

It took a few moments before I could speak.

"Shylo and Toma are one and the same," I said. "I'd like to see him."

She hesitated. "His condition is very serious," she said. "He's had a great loss of blood. Are you related?"

"Yes," I said. "He's my son," and went up to see him. He slept while blood drained into his arm. A doctor told me that he would live. Shylo had told him that a hunting knife had been used on him.

He was back on the street ten days later. Setbacks can put an addict right back on drugs again. Not my Johnny Shylo. He's still clean, and I believe he'll stay clean.

When it comes to the business of people who break away, the name Richard Roselli, who is the director and founder of Drug Addiction Rehabilitation Enterprises, D.A.R.E., comes through like a shining ray in the grim world of drugs. If there was anything to be gained from the experience of Richard Roselli, it was the hard fact that you don't ever give up on people. You never write them off as hopeless drug addicts without a prayer of a chance for rehabilitation. I knew Richie and his family for years. He was an addict.

After twelve years of pleading, reasoning and arguing, I managed to convince him to make still one more effort to get himself clean and Richard Roselli rid himself of his drug habit.

It's almost a physical impossibility to spend twelve years trying to get someone to break away from a heavy addiction. There has to be a grain of truth to the fact that I stayed with Richie without giving up on him because of the close relationship that I had with his family. Nevertheless, the thought that remains is that addicts can be brought back into useful lives no matter how long they've been addicted. I take a measure of pride from Richard Roselli and the addicts enrolled at D.A.R.E. who are helping themselves.

Hopelessness and the negative existence of the addict can be fought and conquered. Rehabilitation centers aren't jails. There are people there who genuinely care and who help.

Roselli's struggle and ultimate triumph can only be classified as a monumental achievement. The structure that houses D.A.R.E. on Littleton Avenue in Newark is a modest two-story wood frame house, with a small tomato patch behind it tended by the addicts. The plants thrive and grow strong under sun and rain and man's care.

It is a place that offers comfort and hope, and to me it represents God's practical work. Indeed, it is truly His house.

CHAPTER ELEVEN

Spina said, "There's something I want to ask you, Toma. Our arrest record in gambling has fallen off. Do you believe there's less gambling activity?"

I said, "No. They've just become a little more careful. If anything, it has increased."

"So they're more careful," Spina said thoughtfully. "That's how I see it too."

"Yeah, but they're also more stupid. They push people around, they take advantage of them for a while, and they begin to think they can do it forever. I'm not awed by them. I know who they are. They're dummies."

Spina smiled. "I appreciate your attitude, Toma, but there are too many of these dummies running around the streets."

I said, "Have no fear, Toma is here."

Spina grinned. "Yes, I know."

I went out and hit the street. I didn't have a definite plan. You don't say to yourself, I'm going to comb the city of Newark for all known bookmakers, gamblers and pickup men. That isn't the way it works. I believe that you have to get out onto the street where you suspect the action is and try to pick something up out of it. You try a location, and if you don't spot anything you move on. You just don't sit on your tail waiting for something to happen. You keep moving, and you hit place after place. You change the odds by exposing yourself to more of what's going on. If you have a good eye for something that's wrong, call it a sixth sense, it can lead you onto something bigger.

It always helps if the hoods don't know who you are. I dressed as a bushy-haired Good Humor man with eyeglasses and a mustache and covered the city in my own car. The break came after three hours, in a bright, narrow little restaurant in Vailsburg. I was at the counter having coffee when I saw two men in a black Electra park.

I knew one of them. They got out of the car, and they looked wrong. It was as though they were acting before a live camera in a third-rate Elliott Ness movie. They wore dark business suits. I thought that black-banded felt hats would have completed the picture. On the sidewalk they stopped, stared into the restaurant, then looked in all directions in an exaggerated attempt to appear casual. And yet it was practically an effort to be noticed by their arrogant and threatening posture. They came in. I've seen thugs enter diners and intimidate people with that stupidity.

The proprietor was a round little man who sat behind his cash register at the front of the restaurant. He paled perceptively when he saw them. I knew the larger of the two men who'd come in. He was Joe Colebrook, and he worked for Casatelli. He was a massive man with a ponderous belly. He grinned at the frightened man behind the register and said, "Hello, Leon, how you been?" in a warm, friendly tone.

"I called," the proprietor said seriously. "Did they tell you that I spoke to them?"

"Yeah, I know about that," Colebrook said.

His partner was smaller, wiry. He stood near the door in a schooled deadpan manner.

"They said they'd give me a little more time," Leon whispered.

"I know," Colebrook said reassuringly, "but I'd like to talk to you. I want to discuss it."

Heads turned. There were six patrons at the counter. Four of them stood up wordlessly, paid and walked out. An old man at the end of the counter gave his attention to a bowl of soup. Behind the counter the short-order cook busied himself scraping the grill. The counterman washed glasses with great concentration.

"Let's talk privately," Colebrook said. "In the back for a minute."

Leon got off his chair and went back and pushed through swinging doors into the kitchen with Colebrook following him. A few seconds went by, and I heard the unmistakable sounds of fists delivering violence, twice.

Leon's employees made no effort to go to his aid. I stood up and went toward the kitchen.

"Hey, Good Humor man, wait a minute," the thin man called. He approached. "Where you going?"

I pointed. "I was just going to use the can."

"The can's closed. There's something wrong with the plumbing. You better try another place."

I said, "Sure." As I was dropping change near the register, Colebrook came out of the kitchen. I left without a backward glance. Outside, I noted the Buick's license number. I went back to my car and got behind the wheel. Leon's visitors left.

I was parked close. I slid down on the seat. There was a chance that thed look around as carefully departing as they had when they arrived.

The Good Humor hat and jacket came off, and the bushy wig, mustache and glasses. When I sat up, I wore an Army surplus work jacket and an engineer's helmet, and I had an unlighted cigar clenched between my teeth.

They were already out in the stream of traffic. The thin man was driving. I turned the key and waited until there was greater distance between us. Colebrook looked back suddenly. He saw nothing suspicious. He turned and faced forward. I got on their tail, keeping three cars between us.

They drove too carefully. They slowed down well before they came to intersecting streets that had traffic lights, anticipating the change. They proceeded in the manner of a very drunk man who was overcompensating by driving too slowly and too carefully, so as not to have an accident and in no way to attract the attention of police because of any reckless action.

My impression was that the car was "dirty," meaning that they were carrying something of an illegal nature. I imagined what the cause was for Leon's beating. It had all the earmarks of an ordered attack by a loan shark who hadn't been paid on time. Leon had received a small sample of greater punishment that could be in store for him.

Arresting Casatelli's musclemen would have meant nothing. I wasn't an eyewitness. I hadn't seen the beating in the kitchen, and I suspected that Leon would be too frightened to name anybody.

Their destination was a grimy four-story tenement over a grocery store at street level on Elizabeth Avenue. Most of the buildings on the block were in the process of being razed. The buildings on the other side of the street had already been leveled. There were only a few cars on the street. A deserted block doesn't afford good cover. Colebrook got out and went into the grocery store while the driver remained in the car.

I turned right into a side street and stopped. I removed clothes from the suitcase on the front seat next to me, and within half a minute I had disguised myself as a wine-soaked derelict, in a scraggly wig and filthy red-plaid flannel shirt. A bottle of muscatel protruded from my rear pocket.

When I turned the corner, the grocery store seemed to be doing a brisk business. A good number of customers seemed to be coming and going. None of them were carrying packages. They could have purchased cigarettes or cigars and pocketed them, but I doubted it.

Colebrook's partner didn't pay any attention to the unsteady wino who came toward him. I went in and determined that the store had to be a front for a policy operation. The shelves were almost bare. A few boxes and some canned goods had yellowed with age. Four men came out of a back room and began walking toward the store's entrance. A fat man with a cigar frowned at me over the counter. "What do you want, bud?"

I swayed. "Could you give me a little help, Captain? I need a little money for bus fare." I pointed at a partially destroyed building on the street. "I was sleeping over there, and some bums came along and swiped my money. I just need enough to get home."

He gave me a hard stare and snarled. "I ain't giving you any money so you can drink with it. You ain't gonna get drunk on my dough."

One of the four men said, "Hey, Pete, why don't you give the guy a break?" He laughed, "How's he going to get home?" He threw me a quarter, and I caught it, in the midst of great laughter.

"Thank you, Captain. I really appreciate it. Good luck to you and God bless you."

There was no sign of Colebrook. I attempted to delay my departure by striking up a conversation with the man behind the counter. I said, "Hey, Pete, what do you think? You think the government is going to send them astronauts up to the moon again?"

He deliberately puffed a cloud of cigar smoke toward me. "Who gives a shit? They ought to send you to the moon and leave you there. I don't want any stumblebums coming in here and panhandling." He jerked a thumb toward the door. "Out! Take a walk."

I mumbled, "Just trying to be sociable."

He reached under the counter and showed me a police nightstick. "Take a walk or I'll break your ass."

I went across the street and made a show of finding cigarette butts until I saw Colebrook leave the grocery store.

I went around the corner, and when they were out of sight, I ran to my car. Tailing somebody who is parked on a different street from the one you're on can be treacherous. You can lose him quickly if he makes a U-turn and heads back in the direction from which he came. I turned the car around, pulled the wig off my head and got to the corner as the Buick went by.

Tailing someone can be an art. He can be observed from almost any direction, including either side, if he's on foot. He can be watched in the reflection of plate glass store windows on the opposite side of the street and you don't have to face him.

Following two guys in a car who might be on the lookout for a tail can be difficult when you're on a street with light traffic. I remembered the way Colebrook had glanced back to check the street after leaving the restaurant.

I followed with a two-block cushion. Traffic lights can become a problem with that distance between the lead and tailing car. A two-block cushion isn't standard police procedure.

It has a number of faults, but the biggest one is getting stopped by lights and the only way to continue the tail is to jump the lights against the traffic. Hitting the siren button is out for the obvious reason that you can be overheard. I listened to screeching tires, screeching people and some strong cursing for about two miles. When you cut through a line of moving traffic, you count on the fact that people are going to see you and slam on their brakes. You hope they'll stop in time.

A daydreamer in a battered old pickup truck didn't see me until he was right on top of me. At the last second he hit the brakes, skidded and plowed into my right front fender.

I yelled, "Sorry," and continued. As I said earlier, the car is a '63 Valiant with over 100,000 miles on it. There was a sentimental attachment. I wasn't going to worry about it. In the mirror I could see him get out of the truck and wave a fist at me. He scrambled back into the truck and took off.

The commuter rush had started, and I had to narrow the distance between the Buick and myself. Cars around you can provide excellent cover. Using a four-car cushion, I changed into the disguise of a Catholic priest. They slowed, trying for a parking slot on Twelfth Street. The block appeared solidly parked with cars.

I turned in to a gas station and left the car with a pleasant gas station attendant after I'd told him about some poor soul who needed help on the block and I just couldn't find a parking spot.

"Of course, Father," he said. "Just leave it. It will be safe here." I thanked him and went down the street in time to see the men I'd been watching step into an apartment building. I broke into a run.

When I opened the street door, they were stepping into the elevator. I waved, "Hold it, please."

Colebrook held the door for me, and I thanked him. When his accomplice pressed the button for three, I hit four. They alighted at three. Before the elevator door opened completely on the fourth floor, I bounded through and galloped down the service stairs to the floor below. I cracked the door leading to the floor and caught a glimpse of them entering an apartment.

I walked over to the door, listened and heard phones ringing for a few minutes. I took a walking tour of the building. There were four floors, and I went through them quickly and heard nothing. The street level had a door that led to the basement. Off a corridor there was a room that held a boiler and three washing machines. Another door at the far end of the corridor was covered with heavy sheet metal. I listened and heard nothing. I pressed my head against the door and listened, and then, using a listening device, I heard the faint ringing of telephones. I guessed that the room had been insulated.

You don't try doorknobs. When people have already gone to the trouble and expense of installing metal doors and insulating rooms, a wired door could be part of the package. Try turning the knob and maybe a little buzzer goes off to alert people. I'd heard enough. I departed quickly by a basement door that led to the street. I made my way back to the gas station and drove the car off. This time I found a slot about five cars lengths behind the parked Buick.

I had no idea how long Casatelli's men would remain in the building. They'd already spent more time than they had at the grocery store while making that pickup. A priest sitting by himself in a parked car isn't going to attract too much attention. Casatelli's men had already seen me in the building. I removed the three-cornered hat and the rest of the disguise and changed again.

I wore a tan sweater and a longshoreman's round wool hat. Patience is part of it. Twenty minutes went by without a sign of the men in the building. I got out of the car, lifted the hood and tinkered with the engine. Suddenly they appeared on the street. They'd left using the same door I had exited from to get back to the street. It was clear that the apartment on the third floor and the room in the basement were both part of the same operation. This time Colebrook drove, and I was behind them again. He deposited his partner at an indoor car park building in Newark and left.

His partner came flying down the ramp in a red Porsche without regard to pedestrians on the sidewalk and went zipping through town. He headed toward the suburbs. He drove onto a brick driveway, and a beaming woman in a white tennis outfit and three small boys came bouncing out of the backyard to greet him.

I thought about going home and calling it a night. Instead, I went back to the precinct. The feeling persisted that the setup could be a large operation. I made a call and got a make on the thin man. They don't always do it, but hoods usually register their cars in their wives' names. The automobile was registered to him, and the name that went with the license plate was Paul Rittman. I made another call and learned that he was a two-time loser in the state of New York for armed robbery. He'd done time on both. The department had already established that he was currently employed by Fred Casatelli.

CHAPTER TWELVE

Outside, the exodus from the city was at its height. The people who had toiled and scurried back and forth in the quest of the buck had departed for home. I thought of the restaurant keeper who was being pressured by loan sharks. After tailing the loan sharks, I'd determined that they were also part of a gambling setup. There was nothing unusual in that. They were both a natural tie-in. I walked and tried to sort it all out. Questioning Leon, the restaurant owner, wouldn't help. In all likelihood Leon was already frightened. He had received hard lumps at the hands of a hood, and he would not be willing to discuss his problems with police. A victim rarely will at the beginning. Later, perhaps if he had a leg broken or thugs calling at his home and smacking his wife around, it could be a different matter.

I'm not a calm man. I've got a lot of nervous energy. I can't sit still. Occasionally my eyes twitch when I'm under strain. And occasionally I talk to myself. It gives me a built-in audience. I said aloud, "Okay, Toma, you're certain that you've uncovered a loan shark and gambling ring. Now why don't you be a good fellow—No, I'll change that. Why don't you be a good cop and take what you've learned and give it to Kendricks? That's what you should do."

"That's what you think I should do," the other me replied. "What do you think will happen if I give it to Kendricks?"

"Oh, that's easy. He'll probably order a special detail for this gambling operation, and he'll see to it that other cops will be apprised of the loan shark pressure that's being applied to Leon. That's a different department, but you probably know that."

"Sure I know that, you dummy. But what you don't know is that I know Kendricks. I know how he thinks. The minute I tell him what I know he's going to send twenty cops over to that building, and he's going to order them to break doors with sledgehammers and crowbars. He'd use tanks if he had them. Tell him about Leon, and he'll send guys over to question him. And leon just might panic at the unexpected intrusion of cops and blow the whole bit. So don't be stupid. Don't be advising me to see Kendricks. If twenty cops go over there and start knocking doors down, all they're going to find is some telephones and a table and an adding machine. By the time they get inside all the gambling slips will be destroyed."

"There's no reason to be belligerent. I don't go for you calling me stupid and dummy."

"You're right. You want an apology? Okay, I apologize."

"Watch yourself."

"I said I was sorry, didn't I?"

"You've obviously chosen to disregard my advice. Now may I ask you how you intend to proceed on this case?"

"I have to think about it. You caught me cold. How would you go about it?"

"I've already told you to confront Kendricks with the facts. But knowing you, you'll probably try to learn as much as you can before you decide to hit them."

"For that the man wins a good cigar. That's the first thing you've said that makes any sense."

"Very clever, Toma. Suppose things change. Suppose they move from that location, then what have you got?"

"Why should they move when they've got a good thing going for them? Okay, so what's my next step?"

"Who knows?"

"I'll tell you who knows. I know. Those gambling guys are also loan sharks, right?"

"Absolutely."

"Okay, I'm tired of talking to you," I said. "I know what I have to do."

To learn about loan sharks, you talk to people who have been victimized by them, or you can talk to hoods, informants and other scoundrels who feel they have something to gain by revealing bits of information, or you can talk to somebody who owes you a favor. Grabowsky owed me a favor for helping his kid brother, and Grabowsky hung around Winters' Poolroom. It was a front for a loan sharking operation. He could feed me some information about the competition. The time was right to call in the favor. I called Winters' Poolroom. He wasn't there, and no one knew where he could be reached. I got on the phone again and called everybody who might possibly know his whereabouts. I called hoods, informants, bartenders, prostitutes, con men and gamblers. After about fifteen minutes I got a bite from Ken Baraty, the bartender at a go-go place called the Inferno.

"Yeah, Toma, he should be here tonight. He's usually in on Wednesday. Yeah, I'm sure of it. He's got something going with one of the girls, and she's working tonight."

The Inferno was a small, shabby store with a fake brick front and a small unwashed window. A large red neon sign hung over it, and on the window a smaller blinking green neon sign advertised go-go girls. Under dim lights the Inferno was crowded. Patrons with their backs to the bar faced a small platform where an Oriental topless dancer gyrated wildly to a jukebox tune.

At the far end of the room black velvet drapes provided a background for a small piano set on a platform. A thick blue cloud of cigarette smoke hung like a low ceiling. Baraty was busy pouring drinks. I headed for an open slot at the far end of the bar. There was a perspiring heavy guy with a buxom redheaded B girl who rested her breasts on his arm and another man who appeared to be alone. I found a slot between them.

When Baraty came over, he said, "He's not here yet." He stared at the Oriental dancer. "That's nice, huh?"

"Beautiful," I said. "Mike has got good taste."

The man who was alone said, "Scotch on the rocks," to Baraty.

"I'll have one too," I said.

"Since when do you drink?" Baraty asked.

"I'm here. I'm taking a spot at the bar, the boss is entitled."

The redhead tapped her glass. "I'll have a refill, Ken."

And the man with her said, "Yeah, hit me again."

Ken hurried off. I watched him pour three legitimate drinks. Then he reached under the bar for a bottle filled with tea. He poured from it. It was the drink he gave the redhead. Baraty set the drinks down, and she downed hers in one swallow.

"I'll have another, Ken," she said.

Baraty gave her a warning look, as if to say that she was getting her companion's money too quickly.

"That'll be five dollars," Baraty said.

He protested. "Five bucks!"

The redhead applied a little more pressure with her breasts and casually dropped a hand to his thigh. "Come on, pay the man," she said. "What the hell, it's only money. We're having a good time, right?"

He dropped a fiver and peeled off a buck for Baraty. "Take it easy. I'm going to be here all night." He laughed. "At the rate she's drinking you guys are going to run out of tea in the kitchen." He knew he was being taken, but he wanted to be taken at his own speed.

It's like the gambler who is told that the crap game is crooked and he replies, "Yeah, but what the hell, it's the only game in town," and so he plays.

I ordered a Coke, and when the guy who was alone on my right was busily engrossed with the go-go dancer, I poured my scotch into his glass.

Whiskey and I don't get along. One or two shots is all it takes for me. While I waited for Grabowsky, a man came up to me and said, "I don't mean to disturb you, friend, but ain't you Dave Toma, the guy who's been in the newspapers with all those disguises?"

"I'm afraid so," I said. We shook hands, and then he asked for my autograph.

Baraty came over grinning. "See that, you're a celebrity, Toma."

Within two minutes everybody in the bar had been informed that Detective Dave Toma, the celebrity, was here.

When the go-go dancer finished her number, a few patrons came over and shook my hand. A burly guy with a cap covered with teamster buttons came over and glowered at me. "You Toma? The guy in the papers?"

I nodded unhappily.

"You don't look that tough to me."

I sighed. "I'm not." He was the upstart in the classic Western film about to show the sheriff up. "I'm not a tough guy." I smiled. "I'm a musician. Come on," I said. I got off the barstool, and he accompanied me to the piano. I did some spot improvisations. He requested a tune, and I played it for him while he grinned happily. We were friends. I sat there for about ten minutes until the jukebox went on again. A different go-go girl went into her act. I went back to the bar and waited for over an hour, and Grabowsky still hadn't come.

The Oriental girl went on again, and when she finished her stint, I asked her if she had any idea where Grabowsky was. She didn't and told me that she was also waiting for him.

I marked the evening as an idea that had gone by the boards and left.

Outside, the air was foul with the stagnant odor of the river and the industrial pollution that had drifted in from some of the oil refineries. It was a good night to go home. Tomorrow was another day. I'd catch up with Grabowsky, possibly at Winters' in the morning.

I began to walk toward the car. They came up to me silently. I didn't see where they sprung from. They stood close on either side. The one on my left said, "Hello, Toma. We've been waiting for you. Keep it cool."

I glanced down and saw the knife in his hand held an inch from my ribs. He was tall, thin and hatchet-faced. His partner was shorter, wide-shouldered. He had a flattened nose and some scar tissue around his eyes that could have been acquired in the prize ring.

From my right his partner whispered, "One smart move, you son of a bitch, and I'll blow your head off right here in the street. Try for your gun and you're dead."

"Walk ahead," the hatchet-faced man said. "There's a little alley right at the end of the building. We'll have a little talk."

I hadn't observed any alley when I had first arrived at the Inferno, but I hadn't been looking for an alley. Faint light from an apartment above the Inferno illuminated a small storage place containing garbage cans and empty beer cases.

The thin man spoke again. "Let's get going, Toma." The voice was quiet with no sense of urgency. It belonged to a man who thought he had full command. He was going to talk me into getting killed. I sensed it.

I said, "Wait a minute. What's it about?" I said no more when his hand came out of his pocket with a gun. I stood with my heart banging on my ribs.

I had the feeling that it would be all over for me if I stepped into the alley. It was like the sick feeling of sitting in a car and knowing with certainty that you're going to have an accident within the next half second.

On the great big silver screen the man in the middle reaches out with both hands and yanks his flankers together with a resounding crash. Or else he drops to a crouch, beats the bad guys to a draw, knocks them off and walks away. Forget it, Toma. You're dead if you try anything.

I slowed, shifting my weight for an instant. I was going to turn my back on the man with the knife and try for the man with the gun. The gun lifted and aimed at my heart. "Go ahead, Toma. I'll blow you away."

We went into the alley, and they dropped back a step. Anybody else would have relieved me of my gun. They were professionals. They were that sure of themselves.

"That's far enough. Don't turn around," the thin man said. "So you're the hero who's getting all the publicity. The master of disguises." He paused. "You're dangerous, Toma. Cops hear about you, and they read about you, and maybe they get ideas that they'd like to try the disguises themselves. You think you're a hero. Heroes are dangerous. They give people ideas."

I started to turn my head.

The thin man said, "Don't. Do you know your trouble, Toma? You don't play by the rules. We're both in the business, and we have to follow certain rules. We don't like to be framed. If you're going to catch us at something, you've got to catch us right. Like that we march off to the can without a squawk. Do you know why I'm telling you all this, Toma?"

"I've got an idea," I said.

"I want you to know why we're here," he said. "I'll spell it out. If you play the game by the rules, you don't get hurt. You ignore the rules by using those disguises. We wind up looking foolish and stupid. You're the one who's going to feel foolish and stupid."

There was a small sound like a shoe scuffling on concrete. Instinctively, I dropped, trying to change position. I jerked my head to the right. It wasn't enough to avoid the butt of the gun. Pain tore through my head, my knees sagged, and I went down on all fours fast. It had been a grazing blow, but solid enough so that the two forms appeared as though in a heavy fog.

I didn't see the shoe that kicked my ribs. There was pain. The impact lifted my body. I caught another shoe from the other side and pain tore through me again. I was being torn apart with it. The terrible realization that they were going to stomp me to death was overwhelming.

On the ground helpless, it could happen like that. I lunged forward and spun around, and I could see both figures crouching. I could make out the gun. We were no more than five feet apart. They waited, challenging me to make an attempt to draw my gun.

Behind them, at that instant, I caught a glimpse of the bulky form of the truck driver I'd seen in the Inferno. He lifted a garbage can over his head and threw it.

It hit the short man's back and his head. He went down as though he had been hit with a construction crane. The sound the garbage can made resounded through the alley. The man with the knife spun around. We both had a momentary glimpse of the truck driver's departure.

I went for my gun. The thin man was very quick. Before I could aim, he kicked my arm, and the gun flew from my hand. He slashed at my face and missed by no more than a few inches. It was happening too quickly. I was still down. I got to my feet. When he lunged for me, I kicked him in the stomach.

Lights were being turned on in the apartments over the alley. I heard a woman scream, "They're killing somebody down there!"

The man who had been hit with the garbage can retrieved his gun and aimed at me again. It's over, I thought. I'm dead, he's going to finish me. I'm never going to see my wife and kids again.

Apartment lights began to come on. He steadied the gun. An empty milk bottle thrown from above crashed and sent glass flying, narrowly missing the man with the gun. It distracted him. The gun blasted fire, and the shot went past and slammed into a garbage can. I attributed his poor aim to the garbage can that had downed him.

From above there was more screaming. More bottles showered down. He fired again and missed, and the bullet ricocheted off the wall. I grabbed the can that had hit him and threw it at him. The third bullet he triggered smashed into the can in midair.

They turned and ran. They were gone from the alley when I recovered my gun. From above somebody was shouting obscenities into the night. "Get out of there, you fuckin' bums." More bottles came crashing down and some bags of garbage.

I ran about six steps, and my legs buckled, and I fell and went down on my face. The kicks to the ribs had taken my strength.

I heard an engine roar into life. When I got to the street the car was moving. I thought I saw a New York license plate. Tires squealed as it turned the corner. They were gone. Pain in my ribs slowed me as I ran for my car. I gave it up. They could take too many directions.

Now that the gunfire was over, some of the Inferno's patrons had stepped out into the street. I went in and asked questions. A man volunteered that he had seen a car with out-of-state plates parked at the curb. It could have been a Pontiac or a Mercury. He wasn't sure. Baraty and the rest had never seen the truck driver, and nobody knew anything about the two thugs who had waited for me. If they did, they were unwilling to discuss it.

I owed a truck driver I had never seen before this night a favor. Nobody knew him.

Baraty said, "It's the first time he ever stopped here, Toma."

I'd skinned my face when I fell in the alley. I washed my hands and face, and as I stepped back into the street, two squad cars entered the block and raced toward the Inferno.

A doctor at Newark Hospital poked my ribs and gave me a cheerful, professional smile. "They're badly bruised, but they're not broken. You're lucky."

I said, "Thanks," and left. I limped to my car and rolled toward home. I thought of the doctor's observation that I was lucky. I kept telling myself how lucky I was. I congratulated myself for having befriended a stranger with Teamster buttons.

A sudden sense of depression and then anger caught up to me. Imagining what had really happened back at the Inferno wasn't difficult. I'd spent two hours at the bar and at the piano. People had recognized me. That had pleased me. We all seek recognition. It's nice to be liked. Somebody had set me up at the Inferno. It could have happened like that. Somebody back there hadn't liked me. He made a phone call, and two professionals had come to do a bloody job on me. I didn't think that they wanted to kill me. Getting stomped by two men who knew what they were doing could have accomplished nearly the same thing. They wanted to teach me a lesson. I'd incurred an intense dislike from somebody, and he'd ordered the beating. They were deliberately unhurried. They wanted me to realize why I was getting my lumps. They didn't need any heroes and cops getting ideas about becoming heroes.

I'd never seen either of them before. If they were locals, I would have known them. Newark isn't that big. There was another possibility. The car had New York plates. I'd waged war against organized crime, and it had made headlines and received national coverage. Organized crime isn't exactly reserved exclusively for the state of New Jersey. There might have been a meeting between top crime figures, and somebody could have brought up the name of a Newark detective who had been cutting into revenue by busting gambling banks. It would fit like that. Fix this upstart. Let him know who's boss. See to it that he's broken and crushed, more dead than alive, and they'll all know who's boss.

The trouble could have come from a number of directions. Before I'd gone to the Inferno, I'd phoned various informants. Somebody could have known that I'd wind up there and seen to it that the wrong people would be told of my movements. I doubted that Baraty had set me up. He had no way of knowing whether or not I had told anyone that I was going to be there. That would have brought it right back to him.

What bothered me was that Grabowsky hadn't appeared. Somebody could have told him that I was looking for him. He could have set me up easily if he wanted to. He had no reason for it.

Exhaustion overtook me on the way home. When I got there, Pat was still awake. She stared at my face and whispered, "What happened, David?"

"I was chasing some kid and I tripped over something."

She watched me ease gingerly into a chair. She sat still for a while. "They hurt you, didn't they, David?"

I tried to keep it light. "Who's they? I told you I was chasing a kid, didn't I?" I said with an annoyance I didn't feel.

I didn't fool her. All the questions she wanted to ask remained silent in her eyes. A policeman's wife also pays a price. She worries about her husband, and her family, if anything should happen to him.

I didn't sleep well that night. I got out of bed and paced. It had been a bad, ugly scene at the Inferno, and it had been very close. I left the lights off and stared out at the little Valiant on the quiet street. There had been threats phoned into the precinct. I had partners who made jokes about driving with me. "Go ahead, Toma. Step in and start it. I'll wait for you, and if you don't go up with a boom, then I'm your partner."

I prowled through the darkened house and saw my slumbering children. Jimmy, Patty Anne, Donna and Janice. They appeared vulnerable. I could see no one in the woods behind the house. There were questions I had to ask myself, and I was avoiding them. They had walked me into an alley, and it had been easy for them. They could have me in their sights whenever they wanted to. You've been careful, but luck had something to do with your still being alive. You've scored points with the Bureau of Investigation, and the newspapers have taken up the cry of the unorthodox cop with unusual methods. A cop who knows compassion for junkies and prostitutes and the poor, all the victims. Was it a wish for fame? What pushes you? Is it a wish to defend the oppressed? Who the hell appointed you Don Quixote? Is it the fear of failure that spurs you on and drives you to be number one? That could be the one, Toma. And maybe you know it too.

So you're the man with the most arrests and convictions. How do you measure that against what you have under the roof of your home? You can worry yourself sick thinking about your family.

It isn't as though I'm looking for death. No policeman is. He knows that it can hover nearby. The incidents go back a long time, and when you keep brushing up against it, it becomes difficult to single out a particular instance. Once, on a job with patrolman Joe Murray, there was a very close call. We were both radio patrolmen then, and we spotted flames from a three-story six-family frame building on Bergen Street. We turned in the alarm, and I carried a one-legged man down three flights of burning stairs. I can remember stepping off a staircase and having it collapse in a shower of burning sparks behind me. There is a vague memory of getting to the street and then awakening in Martland Medical Center with an oxygen mask over my face. I stared up at my wife's face. Someone had summoned her, as well as a priest.

They told me that I had nearly died from smoke inhalation. You have to be lucky, and you have to learn by experience. You learn what being a patrolman is by being out on the street and handling different situations. If you handle enough of them, you have to make mistakes. It's inevitable.

There was a time when I was in the ghetto one evening on a

special prostitution detail. I was disguised as a bum. I didn't want to be solicited by any prostitutes. What I had in mind was to catch some people in the act by following them. It was at a time when I had first made detective, and I had just received some good tips about how to avoid entrapment arrests. My idea was to catch a couple in the act.

It didn't work that way. I observed a car with three men attempting to pick up prostitutes on Howard Street. Four prostitutes got in the car. They drove off with me in pursuit. Five blocks away they stopped and went into the first-floor apartment of a tenement. Standing on a crate, I was able to get a glimpse of three nude men and four nude women through a window. That's it, I said to myself, you've got an arrest. Now all you have to do is lock them up. I went in through the street door and knocked on the door. When one of the prostitutes opened the door a crack, I said, "I'm with three of my friends. I lost them and I saw them driving off." She opened the door unhesitatingly, and I went in like gang busters with drawn gun. "Police officer! Freeze! Nobody moves and nobody gets hurt."

Everybody stood stock still for a moment, and then one of the prostitutes, who was about six feet tall, said calmly, "What are you looking to do? Hold us up? What are you going to do with that gun, kill all of us?"

I said, "Take it easy. I'm a policeman. Nobody's going to get hurt."

"Shit, you ain't no cop. Look at how you're dressed. You're just a bum trying something. Go ahead, shoot."

Some of the others took up the cry. "Go ahead, shoot." I thought that they had to be drunk or something. I showed her my shield.

She said, "You take that motherfuckin' badge and stick it up your ass," and with that she leaped at me.

Obviously she didn't care whether I shot her or not. I wasn't about to shoot her or anybody else. As she leaped toward me, as if on signal the others charged me. I was being rushed by seven people. "To hell with it," I said, and ran for my life and got out of there. Back on the street I realized the mistake I had made going in by myself. I should have called for help. Incidents like this have happened to other policemen. You learn by doing the work. I laughed at my own expense and inexperience and never revealed it to another policeman.

There was a time when I was crossing a street and two men I had arrested a week earlier tried to run me down. I had just stepped off the curb, and I heard the car before I saw it. There was a split-second glimpse, and I dove for the sidewalk. There wasn't time to associate it as an attempt on my life. There was just the car hurtling toward me.

Truth is often stranger than any fiction. It doesn't always work the way it's portrayed in films, where the would-be murderers make the attempt to run somebody down, miss their intended victim and take off burning rubber.

Oddly enough my first impression was that the driver of the vehicle was probably drunk. The mind can trick you. It can refuse to accept the possibility that someone is really trying to kill you. What fooled me even more was that the car had come to a screeching halt after it missed me. Then the driver backed up. I thought he had stopped out of concern. I ran up to the car and held out my shield to identify myself. I was going to bawl him out for reckless driving. A man seated beside the driver grabbed my outstretched arm and the car roared off dragging me along. I tried to get my arm around his neck and was showered with punches. What saved me was the fact that the street was crowded and the driver couldn't put on speed. He slammed on the brakes in an effort to dislodge me. After a block

I fell to the street. My shield had fallen into the car. They sped away. I drew my gun. There was an opportunity to fire, but there were too many people on the street. The incident left me shaken. Torn and bloodied, I returned to the precinct to report the loss of the shield.

Another instance comes to mind that happened on South Orange and Fairmont avenues. It has always been a reminder that a policeman has to be constantly alert for the unexpected. Detective Nicholas Nicorsia and Lieutenant Scriffignano and I, armed with a search warrant for numbers, were about to knock on a door. When the door unexpectedly opened, there were seven men in a single-file line who were leaving. We had them covered, and a search of the seven revealed nothing. There was no hostility displayed by the first six men in line. In fact, they joked with us while protesting that we had somehow made a mistake. At first glance the thought came that perhaps we had. They were attired in business suits, and there was no visible gambling paraphernalia. Still, the apartment had been under surveillance for ten days, and pickup men had been followed and observed entering the apartment. We had been sure that it was a gambling and numbers drop.

The seventh man displayed a case of nerves. It showed in the anger in his eyes, his posture and the aggressiveness with which he threatened to call his lawyer and his talk that he wasn't going to be pushed around by any cops. There was something different about his behavior that contrasted markedly with the other men. You're never completely sure, but it was there. I was standing next to him. I ran my hand through my hair and with a continuous motion I knocked the dark gray hat he was wearing off his head. Decks of heroin showered to the floor.

Nicosia's black mustache spread wide as he grinned. "What have we got here?" He stuck his gun into his belt, then placed the heroin on a small round table and counted sixty decks. Nicosia said, "And all on top of your head. That isn't nice. You ought to be ashamed of yourself."

I went over and began opening dresser drawers. There was movement. One of the men was reaching behind the couch. As if in slow motion I saw him bring up a sawed-off shotgun. As he swung it toward me, Nicosia threw a desperation punch that caught him on the side of the jaw. It had all happened very quickly. The man and the shotgun fell to the floor, and Nicosia pounced on him.

I looked at Nicosia and nodded my thanks. My hands were trembling. A shotgun blast at ten feet would have blown my head off my body.

You need some luck and good cops backing you up.

You can't take anything for granted. Somebody has to be thanked. When it happens, you're never more aware that the man who backs you up holds your life in his hands. So you thank him and count yourself fortunate.

And once in a while when it has been real close I thank the good Lord himself.

CHAPTER THIRTEEN

Spina called in the morning. He'd heard about the Inferno. I explained what had happened. When I finished, he said, "Who were they?"

"No idea. If they were locals, I would have known them."

"What about the people in the bar? Did you talk to them?"

"Nothing, they were all frightened."

He said, "They could try again."

"It's possible, if they don't think that I'm going to stop. It's also possible they think they threw enough of a scare into me last night."

I felt that they'd try again, and Spina knew it too.

"How long are you going to keep this up, Toma?"

"What do you think?"

"They could blow you away, Dave."

"I know."

"My feelings are mixed on you. I don't want my men getting

hurt. You're beginning to make some headway. Three banks and one drop in no time at all. If you back off now, if they can get you out of the picture by threats and violence, then the whole department loses. They could do it to another cop."

He paused. "I'm responsible for you, Toma, the way I am for every man in the department. I'd feel bad if anything happened to you."

I said, "I know. They weren't trying to kill me last night. They were trying to frighten me off by roughing me up."

"It could be different if they try again."

"They had out-of-state plates. Maybe they won't be back."

"Maybe," Spina said. "You've been hitting them hard. Every time you come up with a bust you impress it on their memory. All it takes is a phone call to bring people in from outside. Some guy you've never seen before can walk right up to you and catch you cold. It's possible that you've got nothing to do with them. They've made object lessons from guys like you. It's happened before."

We hung up. Spina's conversation had left me pensive. Recalling the way I had been worked over had an effect. It made me gun-shy.

I was on my way out of the precinct. I wanted to check out Grabowsky's nonappearance last night. I hesitated before stepping into the doorway that led from the precinct to the parking lot. I'd present a perfect target, framed within the doorway.

There was no use waiting. I knew the risks, and I hadn't done anything to lessen them. I walked down the steps and onto the parking lot and climbed into my car.

It took me twenty minutes to get over to Al Winters' place. When I asked him about Grabowsky, he raised an eyebrow. "Didn't you hear what happened to him yesterday? He had an accident with a trailer truck on the Turnpike."

"When did it happen?"

"About four o'clock."

"At night?"

"Nah. In the afternoon. He's banged up pretty good, got a broken nose and ten stitches in his head."

"What hospital?" I had to be sure.

"Jersey City Hospital is where they took him."

I used the phone and satisfied myself that Mike Grabowsky was there. A girl said his condition was fair.

My ribs were giving me pain. I thought, the hell with it, I was going to soak some of the soreness away. When I left the poolroom, Zappo Klinger was waiting outside for me. He was standing in the doorway of an adjacent store, and as I saw him, he signaled me to come over. He didn't want to be seen talking to me on the street.

He was about thirty-five, a big man with a round gut, a jowly face and a sickly complexion. Zappo spent most of his days and nights inside poolrooms, where he hustled unsuspecting marks into games of pool and any other kind of swindles he could work.

"Toma," he said. "I got to talk to you."

"Sure. What's on your mind?"

Zappo licked his lips. He glanced around furtively. "I saw something happen," and now Zappo's voice trembled.

I waited.

"I seen a guy get killed."

"Murdered?"

"Yeah, he must have been."

"Must have been? Who is he? Who killed him?"

He sniffed nervously. "You ain't going to believe it, Toma."

"Take your time. I'll believe anything you say, Zappo. Take it easy."

"Yeah. You know how I make an extra buck, once in a while?"

"I know some of the ways."

"You know, once in a while I get a hustle going for me, but I ain't worked this one in years. Not since I was a kid."

"Which one, Zappo?"

Zappo looked shame-faced. "You know, the measuring bit. I ain't worked it in years because everybody heard about it and I couldn't get any takers."

"What measuring bit, Zappo?"

"Come on, Toma. Why do I have to talk about it? It's embarrassing."

"You can talk to me. I'm your friend."

"You know I used to make hundreds of dollars measuring."

"Measuring what?"

"Come on, Toma, you know. You know the guys in the neighborhood knew that I had the longest one in the whole state, and they used to bring guys around to measure against me. They didn't have a chance. There were guys around here who made thousands betting on me."

I sighed. "Listen, who was murdered and who murdered him?"

"The guy's name was Raoul. He's the guy who was murdered. And Stash, the butcher, murdered him."

"Stash? The butcher over on Mulberry Street?"

"That's him."

I shook my head in disbelief. I knew Stash. I'd gone to West Side High with him. I didn't believe that Stash had murdered anybody. But when people speak of murder, you listen. "How did he murder him?"

"He chopped it off of him, in the back of his shop, right on the butcher block."

I said, "Ah, shit."

"You don't believe it, do you? I knew you weren't going to believe it if I told it to you straight."

"Where's the body?"

"It ain't there. That murderer, that Stash, took the body away."

"How do you know that?"

"Because it wasn't there when I came to," Zappo explained.

"All right, Zappo. Start at the beginning."

"Yeah, the beginning. I was passing Stash's shop, and I seen Stash. He was behind the counter cutting meat for some broad. So he gives me a wave to come in. When the broad leaves, he tells me that I'm no longer the champeen in New Jersey. He tells me that he knows a guy who's got one that's larger than mine. Anyway, I seen him kill him."

I said, "Take it easy, Zappo. Just tell me what happened."

"All right. He told me about this guy Raoul, and I said maybe he wants to back up that statement with a little cash, like maybe a hundred. It's my cousin, he says, and he's here right now. He's visiting. If you got a hundred, then you got a bet. So I put up the hundred; then he calls some guy out of the back of the shop. The guy was nothing, a skinny, dried-up guy with a handlebar mustache. He's wearing an apron. So this guy Raoul looks at me, and he says that I ain't got a chance. So we go to the back of the shop. We're going to measure out on a butcher block. You first, the skinny guy says. So I lay it all out on the block. Then he rips his apron away and throws this thing up on the butcher block. It was like unbelievable. I never seen anything like it. And while I'm standing there amazed, Stash swings a meat cleaver and chops the guy's dong off. The guy lets out a terrible scream. I saw it and I heard it all. It was terrible."

"And then what happened?"

"I fainted. When I come to, the guy wasn't around and Stash was out front slicing livers. I yelled at him, you killed Raoul. Where is he? And you know what that son of a bitch said? Killed who? What Raoul? So I got the hell out of there. That Stash has got to be crazy. I saw that son of a bitch swinging that cleaver. I wasn't going to hang around there."

"Did you call the police?"

"No. I'm telling you there wasn't a body. If I called them, they'd think I was crazy."

"My car's over there," I said. "Let's take a ride and talk to Stash."

"I ain't going in. I saw him use that cleaver. He could get violent," Zappo said in a frightened tone.

Zappo waited in the car while I went to see Stash. He grinned, and we shook hands. "Toma, how are you? It must be years since I've seen you."

"Yeah, it's been years. Listen, I want to talk to you for a few minutes."

"Any time."

"I just had a little talk with Zappo Klinger."

"Where is he? Where is that conniver?"

"Outside in my car. He tells me that you killed somebody."

"Can he see us now?" Stash asked cautiously.

"No, I'm parked down the street."

"What did he tell you, Toma?"

"Never mind what he said. You tell me what it's all about."

He smiled. "Okay. Two years ago I bought a pool table for my son. I got it down in the basement. Anyway, my son starts shooting pool, and he's pretty good. So one night he's in Winters' poolroom for the first time with a couple of his friends. Naturally Zappo sees that the kid is pretty good, and Zappo goes into his act, like bouncing balls off the table, like he's shooting pool for the first time. Then he asks my kid if he wants to play a game for a small wager."

"So he lets the kid win a few games."

Stash nodded. "Three, each time he makes it a little closer.

The next thing you know he starts winning, and he hustles the kid out of a hundred dollars. The boy tells me about it later, and when he describes Zappo, I knew what had happened."

"He said you killed someone named Raoul."

"What killed? He's alive."

I said, "Where's Raoul?"

Stash turned to face the back of the shop and yelled, "Hey, Raoul," and a skinny guy with a handlebar mustache came out.

"Raoul," Stash said, "I want you to meet Dave Toma. He's a good friend of mine."

I shook hands with Raoul, and he said, "I got to get some orders out," and went back.

"The way it happened," Stash said, "we were making sausages on the machine, and the machine got stuck and made a sausage about a yard long. So I thought of Zappo immediately. He goes by the shop every day. I remembered that clown betting on the size of his dong. And I had an idea. It was a way of getting the kid's money back from Zappo." Recalling it, Stash smacked his hands on his belly and began rocking back and forth with silent laughter. His eyes were closed, and then he began ho-ho-hoing like Santa Claus, and that soon changed into a bellowing sound of laughter. He laughed until the tears streamed from his eyes, and his body shook. When the laughter subsided, I got the rest of the story. He and Raoul had planned it. The sausage had been tied to Raoul's belt beneath his apron. Getting Zappo to agree to the contest had been easy since Zappo had never been defeated. Zappo had only a momentary glimpse of a flying sausage and a swinging cleaver. You believe what you see and Zappo believed that he had seen the genuine article.

"You should have seen him," Stash said. "He turned green before he passed out." The memory broke him up again. He threw his head back and flapped his hands against his sides like a penguin trying to take off into a brisk wind. He made gasping, choking sounds and screaming sounds of laughter.

I left. I'd had enough. I had my own problems. Back in the car I told Zappo that he had indeed been dethroned. What he had seen was an accident. Stash had intended to miss, but he had miscalculated.

"But, but. . . ."

"He was rushed to the hospital while you were unconscious. They sewed it back on," I said. "They can work miracles today."

"Yeah, miracles," Zappo echoed. "You should have seen this guy," Zappo said in tones of wonderment.

I dropped him off, and alone in the car, visualizing the scene brought laughter, and laughter brought pain to my ribs. I went home and soaked in a hot tub.

CHAPTER FOURTEEN

I wanted a better look at the layout where I had followed Colebrook and Rittman. In the morning I went back disguised as a telephone repairman. People running a gambling operation are reluctant to open their doors. I ignored the gambling setup. Instead, I knocked loudly on the apartment door to the left of it. The door opened immediately, as if the lady had been waiting behind the door for the knock. She stopped in the middle of a charge with her arms outstretched. "Oh." She clutched a hand to her throat. "I'm sorry. I thought you were someone else."

At ten o'clock in the morning the lady was something to look at. She wore tiny red shorts and a clinging black see-through blouse, and she was barefoot.

"Yes?" she asked.

"Yes, ma'am," I replied. "Telephone company. If I can just take a look out of your back window. We're having trouble with crossed wires in the neighborhood. We're trying to unscramble them."

She glanced at her wristwatch. "You won't be long? I'm expecting someone."

"I'll be through in a minute." I smiled apologetically. "Will it be all right if I open a window overlooking the backyard?"

"Yeah, open two windows if you like."

"Thank you." I opened one and yelled down into the backyard. "John! Hey, John! Bring the truck around. I think the trouble is out in back. I'll check this floor, maybe we can run it down." They had to hear me in the apartment next door. I shut the window, turned to her and said, "Thank you, ma'am."

"You're welcome," she said and hustled me out of there. I stepped next door and heard the phones ringing. Then I rapped on the door.

There was a "yes" from behind the door, and I bellowed, "Telephone company."

The door swung open, and a tall, slender woman peered at me and said, "Yeah, come on in. I heard you yelling out the window next door. What's going on?"

"Are you having problems with your phone?"

"No more than usual. Once in a while I'll pick up the receiver and I hear another party on the line. That's about it."

I said, "Yeah. That's what we're trying to check out."

Working as a telephone repairman gave me the freedom of movement that I needed in the apartment, but I was under continual observation. One room was locked.

"My daughter is sleeping, and there isn't a phone in there."

There were three phones in the apartment. When the one in the living room rang, she rushed to answer it. "Wait a minute," she said and then turned to me. "How long will you be?" she asked.

"About ten minutes," I said

"Call back in fifteen minutes," she said into the phone and hung up.

I wandered around for a while checking wires and the layout of the apartment. There was one door with a peephole to the outside hall. It had a deadlock-type lock. You turned the knob on the inside to lock it, and it had to be locked with a key from the outside. There was a bump in the red carpeting right next to the door and I imagined that it was an alarm button. If she spotted anything of a suspicious nature through the peephole, then all she had to do was step on the button to alert the operators in the basement that there was trouble.

I have to work it my way. Before I call in state, county or municipal police, I want to know how many doors there are in an apartment, where they lead, what type of locks there are and what the alerting systems and means of escape are from the apartment. Success or failure of a raid can hinge on what takes place within seconds. That's how long it can take for those on the premises to destroy all the evidence.

I removed the back plate from one of the phones and said, "Oh, yeah," as though I had discovered something. "Will you look at this? No workmanship, they're putting things together with spit."

I was in now, but getting back inside her apartment again had to be done without any hitches. I said, "I'll be back in a day or two with some new phones." I shrugged. "They're working, but they're shot. They could go out any time, and you'd be without service."

"I wouldn't want that." She stared at me with a frown. Take the phone service away for hours or even the better part of the day, and that meant betting action lost.

I smiled reassuringly. "Don't worry, lady. I'll do the whole job in less than ten minutes."

"Can you come back tonight and do it? It would be convenient for me if you did it then."

"No, I don't work nights."

She went to her purse and waved a ten-dollar bill at me. "Make it tonight."

"Thanks anyway," I said. "I have a wife who's got a mistaken notion that every time I'm not home when she expects me I'm out fooling around." I nodded. "I'll see you in a day or two."

I left and made my way down into the basement and found the alarm wire that went to the area behind the steel door. Anticipate the unexpected. Cutting the wire might trigger an alarm. It was a possibility. I wasn't dealing with amateurs.

Back at the precinct I checked the listings of the phones with the telephone company and learned from the gas and electric company that the building belonged to a man who resided in California. The bills were paid by a real estate management corporation. The landlord in California was clean. It could be yes or no that he or the real estate company knew that a gambling operation was being conducted in the building.

I drew up a schematic diagram of the apartment, brought it to Spina and told him what I thought had to be done.

He nodded. "Good, good. It makes sense, right down the line. Now here's the way I see it. You had this thing from the beginning, so you handle it the rest of the way. I'll set it up with the county police. They'll furnish any help you need. You give them the details."

I said, "Thank you," and went to work.

A lieutenant named Peterson with the county police stared at me as though I was crazy, after I had drawn a diagram and explained what I had in mind.

He said, "Now let me get this straight. You want my men to wander into the building dressed in business suits and sport jackets and you want them carrying briefcases, attaché cases and boxes of laundry detergent."

"That's it. I want them to look like salesmen, and they wander in, one and two at a time. No more."

The lieutenant said, "From what you tell me about the door in the apartment it won't take any time to just knock it in."

"It could be just enough time for them to get rid of the evidence. You do it my way and we'll come up with the brass ring."

Peterson looked dubious. "I've never been on a bust where the police used smoke bombs and fans."

He agreed to my plan when I said, "How many busts have you worked when the paraphernalia was destroyed before you got through the door?"

He stared at me. "You've explained the layout and what you want done. Okay, I understand that. What I don't understand is how a guy like you who must be outranked by three or four men on this job is laying out the plan."

"How many bosses are you going to have on a job? Next time you find the operation. You call me in when you want to crack it and tell me how *you* want it handled."

"Okay, that sounds fair enough."

The operation went off like clockwork. County and city police infiltrated the building as soap demonstrators. Communication was maintained with the use of walkie-talkies. At a prearranged time a smoke bomb went off in the basement while small fans directed the smoke against the doors. A moment earlier we'd disconnected the outside telephone line. All outside exits were covered. I was in the basement when black acrid smoke began to pour through the passageway. I waited for a moment until I was sure that smoke or the odor of smoke had drifted behind the door. I raised my hands like Toscanini conducting a symphony. Five detectives commenced coughing. I shouted, "It's the boiler. She's going to blow. Let's get out of here!" I signaled, and a detective ran past the door. On the concrete floor his leather heels sounded like a swiftly departing flamenco dancer. We waited. When nothing happened, Peterson frowned.

I placed another smoke bomb against the door and directed the flow of air toward the door. There was the sound of three inside bolts being opened and the door opened as far as the chain would allow. Black smoke under the air pressure of the fan poured into the room. The chain was released, and as the door swung open, I said, "Now!" into the walkie-talkie. It was the signal for a man upstairs to knock at the door as a telephone man. Through the peephole she'd see a man who held three replacement phones. As the door opened wider, five detectives charged in and met five operators who were on their way out. Two men at a table were busy scooping up money and slips. There were seven telephones. Fifty thousand dollars in lottery, horses and sports play were confiscated.

Tell it to the man who spends an evening at the track or who bets numbers, and he might very easily say, "So what? What's the harm in a little gambling? It gives me pleasure, and it's my money."

I don't disagree with him, unless he's taking table or rent money away from his family. I regret that some of these bettors weren't with me when we pulled the raid on this operation on Twelfth Street.

At the rear of the apartment there were two locked steel doors. They yielded before sledgehammers and crowbars. Behind those closed doors there were stolen fur coats, television sets, cameras, men's suits, leather coats and ladies' dresses, expensive perfumes and jewelry. It was impossible to see it all because the rooms were solidly packed to the ceilings.

There was a pattern, gambling paraphernalia totaling millions of dollars and two enormous rooms loaded with stolen goods. Here was the proof. It was an enormous gambling setup that could only exist as part of organized crime, and it was also part of a stolen ring and fencing operation. Organized crime provided the outlet for the stolen merchandise, and it was responsible for most street crimes of violence. Bust organized crime, and you take the profit out of stealing. A thief won't steal unless he can take the stolen merchandise and turn it into cash. He can't do it without help from organized crime. It took three vans to haul the stuff away.

Later, in Spina's office, I remember his gleeful expression and him saying, "This is great, great. We knocked them right on their ass." He got up from behind the desk and began walking around, talking as much to himself as he was to me. "You know Toma, I've been a cop a long time. I've never run into another one like you. You're a rebel, but when you're left on your own, you manage to get the job done and you come up with quality arrests. Maybe it works because it's the type of operation that requires one man and it allows him to get in close so he can do damage. It could be. I've seen you make it work. In time all major cities are going to have squads of undercover cops using disguises. It has to happen. You've got some friends. Somebody came down from the London *Daily Express,* and Inspector Irving Moore told them you were a fantastic cop who came up with the idea of using disguises and making them work. The hell of it is that a police department can't work with its men on an individual basis. It isn't practical; it creates jealousies, talk of favoritism." He paused. "There are exceptions to the rules. Some guys are better when they work alone. I know it, and so do Parkinson, Reilly, Dougherty, Zizza, Corrao, Cotle and Foley. They don't all agree on the wisdom of all the wild things you've done, but they all agree that you're the guy who works better by himself." He nodded. "Okay, you've got what you want. You're on your own."

It was as though a heavy weight had been lifted from my shoulders. I was responsible for myself alone.

To know a policeman, you have to swim in his water. He's a man who can be injured or killed by just doing his job, and it can even happen when he's off duty. He is a man whose job entails protecting the lives and property of other people. The price that sometimes has to be paid to keep the streets safe comes high because he can pay for it in injuries and even his life. He's rarely paid commensurate to his risk.

The policeman puts his life on the line. I've been injured thirty times as a uniformed policeman and detective. Some injuries could have been fatal. I've been kicked, stomped in the face and had teeth knocked out. I've had more narrow squeaks than I want to think about. Ask a radio car policeman who's been involved in high-speed pursuit who has an accident what it's like, and usually he'll say, "God was smiling on me," or "I was just plain lucky."

As for myself I'll take any kind of help I can get from either direction.

Live through a riot, and you'll always remember the tragedy. I was at home when the Newark riots of 1967 began. All plainclothes detectives were called in to reinforce the street force. We were put into uniform and assigned police cars. The riot was sparked when a black taxi driver was arrested, and soon a false rumor spread that police had killed the driver. Burning and looting spread. There were four of us in the car. As we rolled into the flame-swept riot area, bullets hit the car like buckshot, splintering windows. Miraculously, none of us was killed. We scrambled from the car to the road with drawn guns, using the car as a shield. We were in the midst of a thousand rioters. A bullet ricocheted off the car's roof, and somebody noted the flash of fire that had come from a rooftop. Another detective and I clambered up the fire escape to flush out the sniper. On the roof bullet fire blasted us. There was no cover. I jumped onto the fire escape, lost my footing and fell to a lower rooftop of an adjoining building, breaking my ankle. The sky was bright with hundreds of fires. I was a stationary target. I dragged myself across the roof and took cover behind a chimney until help came.

I can recall stopping at Don's 21 Restaurant on McCarter Highway in Newark at about two o'clock on a Friday morning, after having spent the evening on a special prostitution detail. My partner was detective Richard Zmijewski. We hadn't seen hide nor hair of any streetwalkers. For some strange unexplained reason it was an evening in which the streets of Newark were completely free of the joy ladies. It can happen that way. It even appeared to those with suspicious natures that somebody had tipped the ladies off and they had all decided to attend the cinema or visit relatives they hadn't seen in years.

It was a quiet evening, and I welcomed it. There was an Italian festival in progress on the parking lot in front of the diner. Brightly colored lights strung overhead illuminated a happy crowd who purchased sausages, pastries and fried doughnuts from the vendors.

Inside the diner there were three police captains. Charlie Zizza, Joe Manghisi, and Rocco Paradiso. We were asked to join them at their table. I sat down, and then unexpectedly a fight erupted in the diner between a group of toughs who were with some young girls and three members of a Hungarian acrobatic troupe. Later I learned that they had come over from

Europe specifically to appear on the *Ed Sullivan Show*. The Hungarians conversed in their native tongue, and the toughs, who had been drinking, decided that this was somehow subversive. They chose the opportunity to impress the ladies with their physical prowess. Their leader walked over to the Hungarians and demanded that they talk "American" like everyone else.

The acrobats understood the word "American," so they smiled and said, "American, American, yes, yes," and they smiled at each other and at the stranger who had come over to their table.

The youth did not choose to view their friendly smiles as such. Instead, he decided that the Hungarians were laughing at him. Whether he genuinely believed it or whether he was attempting to impress the girls at his table was something I was never able to determine.

The stranger pushed one of the seated acrobats, who tumbled over in his chair.

The acrobats were small of stature, but agile and strong. One of them stood up and flattened the stranger with a single punch, and the fight began. Friends of the flattened hero ran to join the battle. Others in the diner chose the side of the acrobats. Within seconds glasses and chairs were flying through the air. Large plate glass windows shattered. The strong man in the acrobat act picked up the cash register and threw it at someone and narrowly missed killing him. I doubt that the fight would have begun if there was one uniformed policeman in the place. The police officers all wore plainclothes. We rushed to intervene, identified ourselves and managed to break up the fight. A number of people had been injured. Some had nosebleeds and blackened eyes. Nobody wanted to make a complaint. Business in the diner was finished for the rest of the night. It appeared as though a tornado had hit. Broken chairs, overturned tables, broken dishes, food, silverware and spilled coffee covered the floor.

Patrons began to file out of the restaurant and mixed with the crowd of spectators from the festival who had gathered because of the fight. Suddenly there was scuffling outside, next to the door. A cart overturned.

I was standing at the door, making my way out when it happened, and as I pushed through, I grabbed one man from behind in an effort to pull him away. I got him back about five feet. I remember yelling, "Cool it." My head was almost torn off. Somebody had punched me from my right side. I hadn't seen him or the thrown blow. I went spinning down and hit my head on the diner stairs.

There were two men. One dropped onto my chest with his knees, the other grabbed my head and began pounding it against the tarred surface of the ground. I managed to bring the hard edge of my hand across the throat of the guy who was pounding my head. He made a gargling sound and disappeared from view.

I reached up for the other man's tie, pulled him toward me and landed a fist on his nose. He flew backward. As I scrambled to sit up, I saw movement behind me. I caught sight of his face and then felt a thrust of fire between my shoulder blades. My face hit the ground hard. I pushed myself up with a vast effort and felt suddenly weakened. I stood up, wavered and stumbled. I heard a woman screaming somewhere.

Zmijewski came over. "Dave, there's blood all over your back." I pulled the sweater over my head. My shirt plastered itself to my back. I couldn't see the man who'd stabbed me. Over near a vendor's stand people were screaming, "He's got a knife."

I drew my gun and went over there on legs that felt as though they were floating. People standing in the presence of a man wielding a knife give him plenty of room. He waved it back and forth to show me that he had it. I held the gun pointed at the ground and held my other hand out toward him. I said, "Give me the knife."

"I'll kill you," he said quietly, but I could sense the fury in his voice. He lunged forward as I approached and stopped when I raised my gun. In the fight back inside the diner, somebody had broken his nose.

A man's voice shouted, "Shoot him. Shoot the son of a bitch. He stabbed you!" Others were quick to pick up the cry.

I said to my assailant, "I'm a police officer. Drop the knife and step back. I don't want to hurt you, and I don't want to shoot you. Now just drop the knife."

"Nobody is going to take it away from me," he said.

We were standing close to each other, and I tried smacking his arm with the heel of my hand and missed. The knife flashed toward my throat. I got back with about an inch to spare.

A mob can be ugly and unthinking. They urged me to kill him. There was a humming in my ears, and I was unsteady. There was an absence of pain. I imagined that I was in shock. I didn't want to be his executioner. If he lunged for me again, I'd have to fire at him. It would be murder. He had already committed his crime. He had knifed me. It had been done. It was not in progress now.

I could feel the world turn under me. My vision began to blur. I started to say something to the man with the knife. I began to fade out. The ground moved beneath me. I yelled for Zizza, and he came running toward me with two other cops. I heard a metallic clank as my assailant dropped his knife before I went into sudden darkness.

I came out of it in a radio police car. I was propped on the front seat between two cops. The siren was on full, blasting my eardrums. There were signs I didn't like. Light cast by the headlights began to grow dim and then brightened and then went dim again.

The cop sitting on my right had something pressed against my back exerting pressure. I heard him say, "Move this thing, he's bleeding like a stuck pig."

I tried to say, "I'm all right," and heard an inarticulate croaking sound instead. The lights went dim again, and I had a sudden fear that they would go off completely and it would be all over. I thought of my wife and children. She'd have a tough time raising four kids by herself. I remember calling her name, and then I could only think that I was sinking into a deep dark pit. I came out of it as I was being carried from the car, suspended by two policemen.

It was determined that the knife hadn't touched any vital organs, narrowly missing my heart and lungs. It was a deep puncture wound. A specialist commented that I had to be the luckiest man in the world because the knife had missed my heart by a fraction of an inch.

Forget that nonsense about knifed television heroes who are hospitalized briefly and are back on the street in no time flat and as spry as they were before receiving the wounds. I had received a concussion which gives me headaches to this day, and the knife wound further aggravated a previous back injury.

In the years following the diner fight hundreds of people have asked me why I hadn't shot the man who stabbed me, indeed, all those who had been in on the attack. I've thought of it many times. It's possible that had I been facing the man when he attacked me, I would have shot him if I had no other means of disarming him. It would have been done in self-defense.

Conceivably, my actions might have been different if he had jeopardized the lives of bystanders in the diner. As a fact, I know that I would not even consider shooting him for breaking up chairs and tables. Anything is possible. He could have been a mental patient, or he might have felt that he was fighting for his life.

Oddly enough, when the case came to court, the latter was the defense that was offered for the two men who had been arrested. One was the man who had stabbed me and the other the man who had knocked me down. It had all happened so quickly. Under the effect of having my head pounded on the ground my vision had blurred, and I didn't want to risk making a positive identification on the others because I wasn't sure of their identities.

Both men were found not guilty. It was a verdict that I never understood. The police who had been involved in the diner fight had identified themselves when they interceded. In view of the large unruly crowd in the diner and the fact that we were all in plainclothes, it would have been inconceivable for them to have acted otherwise.

Nevertheless, the two suspects stated under oath that they were not aware we were police and they were certain that they were fighting for their lives. It was the price a cop can pay, and it occurred when I was off duty. People don't change. I know myself. If the same set of circumstances should present themselves, I know that I would act exactly as I had. There's nothing heroic about firing a gun at another human being, especially when it isn't necessary. It can be difficult when you've been injured.

Ask a cop who's had it happen to him and he'll tell you the same thing. He's not Superman. He's a human being. It's natural for him to retaliate when he's been hurt. And yet the everyday policeman shows a remarkable restraint in the face of an insanity that has gripped the country. He has been gunned down in police stations and on the street by snipers and madmen. He continues to serve. It isn't only his restraint that is remarkable. It's the man himself who serves and puts his life on the line who is a remarkable human being.

I've never fired my gun deliberately but there was one time when it was accidentally discharged. Plainclothesmen James Corrao, George Lepre, Bobie Cotle and I were cruising one evening when we saw twenty-five men shooting dice in an Orchard Street poolroom. They were in plain sight from the street. We went in and identified ourselves as police officers. It meant nothing. There was a mass push of players to get away. Suddenly twenty-five players were charging at us. It was a type of madness. They stampeded. George Lepre and I were knocked down, and my revolver went off, shattering the front plate glass window. It could have been a lot worse. I could have killed someone. Eight crap players escaped, running madly for their lives, and one of them was almost hit by a car as he fled across Bergen Street. It was pure madness. The fines were $10 per man.

CHAPTER FIFTEEN

Because of the reputation I had gained over the years as a quick-change makeup expert and the resultant publicity that had ensued, I've been asked to deliver hundreds of speeches at colleges, high schools and elementary schools, as well as fraternal and religious groups. They were done gratuitously.

It began when ghetto school children who had read of the arrests through the use of disguises wrote requesting that I appear at their schools. A detective who carried twenty-five disguises in his car and who became the actual character that he portrayed was fascinating to them. They all wanted to know how it was done. I explained the reasons for the disguises to them and said, "I don't like to bang in doors unless it's absolutely necessary. I'd rather sneak in without hurting anyone. Break a door down and somebody can get a heart attack. With my disguises I can get in and arrest someone before he knows what's happening. I don't give him enough time to get rid of the evidence. I taught myself to work in front of a mirror, putting on makeup, a scar on my face, and learned how to make myself look shorter, taller or thinner. I can change my complete appearance in a minute. When I become a sixty-five-year-old man, I walk like him. I psych myself up so that my bones ache."

Black kids took a special delight when I described the steps I had taken to disguise myself as a black man. I can remember a bright-eyed twelve-year-old youngster interrupting my speech with the comment "Mr. Toma, you're just trying to pass. But nothing's going to help you. I'd recognize you in a minute." It disrupted the audience and brought peals of laughter.

A rigid disciplinarian immediately hand motioned him to leave the auditorium. I interrupted and asked that he be brought up to share the stage with me. My request brought wild cheering and applause, and the smiling youngster came up. From that moment on that audience belonged to me. I knew the ghetto, and I knew the jargon and how to "rap" with the kids.

I gave speeches to audiences of kids who were hostile. A black boys' club comes to mind. I attempted to convey my thoughts that the overwhelming majority of cops are honest, dedicated, compassionate men, but that they were only human. I always pointed out that man wasn't perfect and there was always the possibility of a bad apple in the barrel the way there would be in any other organization. That viewpoint had been greeted with applause and cries of, "That's it, man. Right on!" You have to give people credit for what they know. You don't try to con kids with the blanket statement that all cops are perfect. They're not, and it's a fact. And if you want them to listen and believe, you say it.

Later, some of the youngsters came to me and asked what the requirements were for becoming a police officer. It was gratification enough for me just knowing that I had made friends for myself, as well as for the department. A drawer filled with notes of thanks from all over the state of New Jersey can make you feel pretty good. One of my biggest thrills came when the members of that young black boys' club voted me in as a director. It has always been a high spot in my life.

During this particular time I was also making a substantial number of narcotics arrests. Witnessing the horror, misery, and waste of life during my daily rounds was a depressing experience.

Anyway, in the middle of a lecture, while discussing disguises I looked out at 800 elementary school children with the sad realization that some of them would eventually become addicts.

I already had their attention. They had listened avidly to all details of my work. They were a captive audience, and I felt compelled to talk to them about narcotics addiction.

I heard a few groans, and then I dropped all pretense and told it the way it was. You don't talk down to them. I told them of addicts and pushers I had arrested, what their physical condition was, what had driven them to drugs and kept them on it. And I warned them about how their own friends would try to get them on drugs. "Everyone has pain, frustration, strains and worries in his life. It's expected, and it's part of living. There's also a time for happiness, but the man who walks around in his life grinning from ear to ear every waking hour of the day figures to be a complete idiot. Life isn't all smiles. So you learn to toughen up and take some of the pain and disappointment that's dished out." I told them that I had faith and confidence in each and every one of them, and I told them that I loved each and every one of them. "Don't let yourselves and the people who love you down." I can remember getting through to them.

Invariably pot and its legalization came up when I lectured at colleges and high schools. They wanted to know my thoughts on it, and I told them. "If a person could smoke grass without being affected, then what would be the harm? If he experienced no reaction, he wouldn't continue to use it. It does have an effect. Nobody can tell me that he can smoke pot and then drive a car normally. I've seen people smoke it who have freaked out and gone right out of their heads. Why would anyone want to walk around feeling stupid, silly, paranoid or frightened to death?"

It always happens, especially on college campuses. I hear the argument that marijuana is less harmful than alcohol. Look at the traffic accident statistics and the broken homes. Nevertheless, the fact remains that alcohol is around, and in most states it's legal. I've spoken to addicts who have been strung out for years. At times when they're lucid I've heard, "Booze is bad enough. Everything is screwed up enough as it is. People don't know anything else to get high on. Can you imagine a doctor, a businessman, bus driver or judge going to work high on marijuana?"

Alcohol has controls. There's a label on the bottle that tells you the proof content. That alone isn't going to cancel out any harmful effects it can have if it's abused. Nevertheless, there is a control over content and potency.

There aren't any controls over marijuana. But I'm not saying that it would be all right to smoke pot if there were controls. There hasn't been enough research done on it. I've seen that it's harmful. Potency and purity and effect are different in grass grown in Mexico, South America, Cuba, Costa Rica. Smoking a joint on one occasion, without any or little effect can be a completely different freaked-out experience on another. And even more dangerous are the pushers and the distributors. It's the unstable nature of the people involved in drugs. I've known of marijuana treated with LSD to increase its potency and hallucinogenic effects. I've seen the body of an eighteen-year-old girl lying at the bottom of an alley after she jumped from a fourth-story window after smoking marijuana treated in that manner. I've seen people after they've smoked marijuana that was dipped in ether. They call it Angel Dust. I've seen them smoke just enough of that to have it affect their minds so that they wind up in mental hospitals like vegetables. It takes very little.

Then the question arises: Who would do anything like that? The answer is obvious. Think of the cruel dealer who traffics in drugs without any regard for human life. That animal would not be reluctant to doctor marijuana in the interest of making money.

Marijuana isn't legal, and those who smoke it have to seek out drug-oriented groups where they're accepted. The odds are high that in a group of drug-oriented people there are some who have experimented with or are using hard drugs.

Proximity has everything to do with it. Associating with dubious people and hard drug users has to pull a certain percentage of marijuana smokers into hard drugs. It's inevitable. People who are high on pot are more susceptible to a suggestion that offers hard drugs.

What always amazes me is that it isn't only students who come up with arguments for the legalization of marijuana. On more times than I can recall the parents of these kids questioned me on my opinions about marijuana and violently disagreed with me after I'd made them known. Because of it, I've been accused of voicing conservative viewpoints. Conservative, middle-of-the-road and liberal thinking has nothing to do with it. Marijuana represents possible hazard to human beings. Nobody flies off a ski jump unless he knows all he can learn about jumping. Without fail the tobacco and alcohol theories purporting that they were both more dangerous than pot were brought up.

Chain smoking never helped anybody's health, and the same thing applies to heavy consumption of alcohol. They are with us. But marijuana is different. We still haven't determined the long-term physical effects. We know that it lowers body temperature, reddens the eyes, changes blood sugar levels, stimulates the appetite and dehydrates the body. It is also reported that the drug accumulates in the liver. The user finds it difficult to make clear decisions. Severe reactions set in with heavy use. Hallucinations, imagining objects that are not there, and delusions, beliefs not based on reality, occur. For some, psychotic reactions occur with the smoking of one cigarette. The belief that marijuana is medically safe isn't supported by medical evidence.

At the present time marijuana is classified as a Schedule I drug, meaning it is considered an abusable drug without any known medical use. There may be theraputic use. Research at UCLA hints that THC found in marijuana reduces fluid pressure in the eye, reversing the pathological condition of glaucoma. In Massachusetts scientists have seen a rare hormonal phenomenon, the development of breasts in some males who have used marijuana. Interaction of marijuana, heroin, alcohol, insulin, barbiturates, and tobacco is also being conducted at various research institutions. In short, we don't know all there is to know about marijuana. In some states its use is a felony that will prevent a person from entering professions such as law, medicine, teaching and civil service.

There is a certain percentage of pot smokers who go on to hard drugs. Don't gamble with the lives of your kids. A parent has to be a parent. Children don't grow up by themselves like trees in a forest. A parent would caution his children about the dangers of crossing a street. And yet I know intelligent people who actually condoned and smoked pot in their homes in the presence of their children. I don't profess to be an all-knowing man, but common sense tells you that you wouldn't put your child's hand into a meat grinder when there is a possibility that he can lose his hand.

The head of a household who allows the use of marijuana in his home is playing with images. Somehow he considers it clever, worldly, sophisticated and "in." It's what he thinks he should be, but it has nothing to do with real life.

Leaders have to set examples. The words "politician," "states-man," "policeman" have got to mean uncorruptible public servant. I'm not awed by a man's position. It's the man, his own self-respect and the extent to which he cares for humanity, that concerns me. One of the advantages of the powerful figures in organized crime and those in high positions is that they can play games with the lives of people. They're stupid, arrogant and contemptuous of people, and inevitably they show their hand. They regard people as objects to be manipulated rather than people.

I'm not interested in the man who takes numbers behind the counter. I want the dummy who stands on top of the heap and whose very stupidity makes him think that he is inviolate from the laws and from the misery that he has perpetrated through narcotics and fast dealing on his fellowman. Over the years I've always said what I believed. It's a good way to live, but you live dangerously. You shake people up like that, and you can incur the wrath of an occasional superior.

Despite the statistics, all crime is not related to drug abuse. Some people are just plain sick, mentally sick. You take a criminal, and he rationalizes. In many cases he actually believes that he is right in what he does. He feels that life has given him a fast shuffle and deprived him of what's rightfully his. He points out swindling and corruption in high places and on a scale that he cannot even begin to undertake. He believes himself to be more in the right than he actually is, and it's this belief that drives him to act more in the wrong. Drugs may have nothing to do with his attitude. He's just oriented to his own particular type of thinking and sense of values. There are people in jail who will always be in jail. They don't want to come out. They don't want to live in the world as it exists, so they make their own little world in jail. For them being in jail means being secure and without the hassle going on outside. There are many facets to the reasons for crime.

In a city like Newark 70 to 80 percent of all crime is committed because of the addict's need to feed his habit. A girl using drugs doesn't care where or how she gets the money.

Her thinking process, outlook and attitudes are completely different from the nonuser. She doesn't think logically. It doesn't enter her mind that if she steals or prostitutes herself, she might go to jail. She's not thinking about going to jail. Her real worries begin when she gets caught, and the panic sets in when she knows she won't be able to get drugs when she's in jail. For the male addict the scene is even a more violent one. He'll rip off, mug, slash, bludgeon and murder.

Education has to be utilized. I don't mean having a teacher telling her class that drugs are bad and letting it go at that. You can't hold an assembly and feel that you have educated children to the problems of drugs. Addicts, former addicts, parents of addicts, professional athletes, medical specialists and educators can help by speaking out. You have to get to the minds of children before they begin experimenting with drugs, and it can't be done by teachers or anyone else speaking to kids from a position of authority. It has to be done from a position of knowledge. People have to learn about drugs. It's difficult to change the established order of things in the academic community, but it would make a lot of sense if a compulsory course in drug education was offered at all schools. I doubt that substituting it for economics would meet with any student resistance. If a situation stinks the way drugs stink, then you air it out. I believe in positive action. You do not remain silent in the face of those who would destroy society with drugs.

There's a belief held today that sniffing cocaine and smoking hash and pot are part of the new culture. I can remember when it was part of the old culture, when muggers, thieves and stickup men used them to bolster their courage. I've seen the bloodied victims.

The drug scene is so far removed from the average household that parents cannot conceive that their children are users. They are often reluctant to admit it when they are. At this very minute I can hear myself talking to a group with the realization that I was not communicating. There was opposition to everything I said. It was in their complacency. Lecturing is an emotional thing. When I step out before a thousand people, I do not have a prepared speech. I begin to speak, and when it's going good, when I reach them, I know it. I hadn't. I grew frustrated and angry.

I can see and hear myself now, talking to that group. "Let me tell you something. You think grass is nothing and it's harmless. I know a young man who believed as you do. He laughed at me when I said that grass was highly unpredictable. For seven years he had used practically every drug imaginable, and he considered grass completely harmless. He smoked it every night. He said I was talking through my hat. That was nine

247

months ago. A day after our conversation he was offered a joint by a guy who described it as a real horse killer. It looked identical to marijuana he had smoked in the past. He took three puffs, and the walls fell in on him. He called his mother and asked her to please come and get him. He said he was sick and couldn't drive. She called me, and we drove out to get him. He couldn't walk to the car. I half dragged and half carried him. He mumbled incoherently and complained that the left side of his body was completely numb and that his tongue felt as though it were three times its usual size. He said there was no feeling in his fingers and his hands. He said that the left side of his head felt as though it were going to explode. His mother became very frightened and rushed him to a doctor, and the doctor, after examining him, recommended a psychiatrist. He found nothing abnormal with his hands, fingers, head and tongue. A psychiatrist diagnosed it as schizophrenia. He was admitted to a mental hospital and attempted suicide by cutting his wrists the second day he was there. He ran into a wall and split his head open. When he was able to speak again, he said that his tongue was much worse. There wasn't any room in his mouth for air. He couldn't breathe. After seven weeks he was released from the institution. Nine months have passed, and he complains that he has lost the feeling in his fingers and that his legs are numb and that his tongue swells from time to time. He cannot function. He has severe headaches. I spoke to him a month ago, and I asked him to tell me the truth. What really happened? What made him freak out? He told me that people don't like to admit that they've been wrong. He was wrong. He took three drags, and it put him into a mental institution and a restraining jacket. What I had told him a year ago had proved to be true.

"I know it isn't a popularly held belief, but nobody knows what grass is all about. Scientific people write consumer reports and say that there's nothing wrong in smoking grass. They walk into a drug rehabilitation center, and they ask questions, and the addicts tell them what they want to hear. They lie to them, because the social workers and psychologists go into the ghetto as though they're doing some kind of survey or paper. You learn nothing like that. Pretend that you're an addict yourself. Ask other addicts what grass is really like, and they'll tell you that they'd rather not use grass because it's unpredictable. You can smoke it for one or two years without its affecting you. Maybe you get a little high. Then one day you use it and you freak right out of your mind, because you weren't psychologically ready for it. It's a fact. One day you're high on two puffs, another day it takes ten, and then maybe the third time you try it you freak right out of your mind. You don't know who you are after you've taken the first puff.

"I know another man who has been heroin-addicted for twenty-three years. Now he is enrolled in a methadone program. He boosts it by drinking wine. He's thirty-five, and he walks like an old man and says that methadone has affected the marrow in his bones and that he has very little sex drive. I look at him and see what he has done to himself, and it's enough to make me sick.

"There are sicknesses that mankind battles daily. Researchers spend their lives seeking prevention and cures. The difference is that drug addiction is a man-made sickness, and profiteers give this sickness to people and profit from their illness.

"There is an unquestioning willingness among people to accept what some scientists believe is the harmlessness in grass. They endanger their listeners with their careless speech. There are as many researchers who see hazard in pot as there are others who see it as harmless. Another group advances the theory that anyone who is opposed to marijuana is somehow restricting a person's freedom of choice to do as he or she sees fit. It has nothing to do with freedom. I don't want to restrict or limit freedom of choice. If we lose freedom, we're all dead. It gives me equal right to fight what I oppose.

"Why should anyone want to take the chance that he or she will not be affected adversely by smoking pot? There is a natural sequence of events for the drug addict, a progression. An addict rarely begins by mainlining with heroin the first time he experiments. Sniffing glue, smoking pot, drinking narcotic cough syrup is where it usually begins. Speed, pills and the rest have to be worked up to. If a man smokes pot and enjoys it, he is in very serious trouble. The trap is his own mental attitude, a way of thinking. He's getting a pleasurable high. It can dull his own natural defenses for self-protection. Somehow he feels a little more knowledgeable than his fellowman. He's gotten over the fear of pot, and nothing has happened to him, so why not take the next hurdle, perhaps something a little stronger? But something happens to him. He's like the kid who steals a set of hubcaps. He gets away with it. He's building up his nerve, and sooner or later he's stealing cars.

"It is exactly the same premise that applies to experimenting with drugs. How can one assume that experimenting with drugs once begun will not become self-destructive? When things are running right in the world for man, he feels that he has control. What guarantee does he have? Marriages go sour, businesses fail, personal relationships go bad, depression can set in, anything can pull a person down. He begins to lean on drugs, and he's pulled into the trap. It is worse than the addiction of alcoholism, and the results are even more disastrous."

I concluded with, "In the name of God, of decency, of common sense, of love of mankind, of anything that you hold dear to you in this world, see it for what it is. I won't give an inch. I won't take a step back. Help me. Join with me and help me fight."

Those were my words, and when I ended, I was shouting for all to hear. I've known scorn and ridicule, but I've also seen thousands of people stand and applaud and I've seen tears. I'm an emotional man, as I've said earlier, and it isn't usual for me to cry with them. I've been embraced by men and women at the conclusion of some of those talks, and I've heard people whisper, "God bless you."

There's no rush to accept marijuana. I say wait until all the facts are in.

CHAPTER SIXTEEN

The restaurant was a fancy dimly-lit place bustling with business. There was a long, padded bar with vinyl-covered barstools that ran along one wall. Facing it was a room divider with a crown of artificial plants. On the other side there was a string of booths, all occupied. The room let into a white-tableclothed dining room. Headwaiters and waiters hovered over tables. Diamonds sparkled in a sea of minks. The scent of delicate pérfume mingled with that of good after-dinner cigars.

The chef, Henri Doran, had arranged the waiter's job for me. He owned the restaurant. It was a real break for me. Henri knew me, and I considered him a friend. Over a five-day period I'd picked up enough information to make two gambling busts. It allowed me to get in real close. It was a place where hoods gathered. When I saw a telephone number being passed at a table, I managed to spill a bowl of salad over a guy and in the excitement caught a glimpse of the number. When I attempted to wipe the salad off his jacket, he threw a punch at me. I checked with the telephone company and got a name, and it led to a numbers drop and a bust.

Two years ago Henri had called me. He was worried about his daughter and had come to the precinct to talk to me. She was nineteen then. It was the man she ran with that Henri feared. He explained his apprehension. He was a man who had worked hard all his life. The young man his daughter was seeing had no visible income, and yet he drove a new Cadillac, wore fine clothes and showered his daughter with expensive gifts. His daughter had told him that the man was wealthy and didn't have to work.

"And you don't believe it," I said.

"No. I've seen men like him in the old country. They never worked, they always had money, and they were always in trouble with the police."

I said, "I understand your concern. There isn't anything that I can do to him unless he has violated the law. Is there anything else you can tell me?"

"Yes. He brought her home one evening and her face was black and blue. He had a bloody nose and a blackened eye. He said that they had been in a drive-in theater, and a group of youths had made some insulting remarks to them, and a fight had started."

"And you don't believe this?"

"I know when my daughter is lying. She resents my concern. I don't want any harm to come to her. You would be doing me a big favor if you could tell me who this man really is."

When he put it that way, it really wasn't that big a favor. It was only natural for a parent to be concerned. I said, "Why did you call me, Mr. Doran?"

"I saw your picture in the newspapers and read that you

made narcotics arrests and that you had addicts in your own family. I thought a man like this will care and will not ignore me."

"You said nothing about narcotics before."

He shrugged. "It's only a feeling. He reminds me of a certain type of person that I've seen in Marseilles and in Turkey who dealt in heroin."

He wanted me to check his daughter's boyfriend out because he reminded him of some unsavory types he had known. Investigations have begun with far less and have become cases. Henri wasn't asking for much. He was worried about his daughter's welfare. He cared. It was a sign of love.

There's a lack of communication. The young want to walk and learn by themselves. That's the way it should be. Their parents didn't want them bruised along the way, and that was also the way it should be. Henri might have had justification for his concern. Somehow the story about the boyfriend and his daughter getting their lumps in a drive-in theater didn't wash.

I told him I'd see what I could learn. He volunteered some additional information. The boyfriend's name was Thomas Zeff. He gave me his description and the make of his car. His daughter had met him at a dance. I took Henri's address, and he agreed to call me when Zeff would show.

"I appreciate whatever you can do, Mr. Toma." He stood up.

I watched him step out into a snowstorm; then I got on the phone and called records and tried to get a make on Thomas Zeff. They had nothing. There were other agencies that could supply information, but I wasn't ready for that step. There was also a chance that Henri's fears were unfounded.

He called me at my home later that evening. His words were hushed. "I heard her on the telephone just a few minutes ago. He's on his way over to pick her up."

255

"How long will that take?"

"About half an hour, I think. That's how long it usually takes."

I told my wife that I had to run. We were in the middle of dinner.

"Right this minute? Can't it wait fifteen minutes?"

I smacked my hands together. "Put some veal Parmesan in between some slices of bread and make a sandwich."

"When will you be back?"

"I don't know. It could be a few hours."

"It could be all night."

"I'll call you," I said, and left with my sandwich. I gulped it down as I drove. It lay like a rock in my stomach. Time was short. I put the brights on, raced along the parkway at eighty-five and had to bring it down when the shimmy in the front end began bouncing me all over the road. It was nine thirty when I found Henri's house. It was a small red-brick bungalow trimmed in white, with a well-tended lawn behind a neatly trimmed row of privet hedge. The shutters glistened with a fresh coat of white paint. The shrubbery showed loving care. I drove past the house, pulled over to the curb, adjusted the rearview mirror and waited.

She came out when Zeff drove up. I tagged them for three blocks without switching the headlights on. We went into Newark, heading toward the ghetto. I disguised myself as a bum. He slowed, looking for a number, and got out in front of a four-story tenement. She remained in the automobile. I parked up ahead and closed the distance between us with an imitation of a drunk. I had to get close to see the apartment that was his destination. The girl sat in the car with the windows up and doors locked. I made a mental note of the license number.

On the shallow wood porch there was a doorless refrigerator

and a rusted swing with mildewed pillows. He was at the front door. He spun around when the porch creaked under my weight. I staggered, cursed and fell. A half-filled bottle of muscatel broke as it hit the porch, and I went into a bitter tirade.

Zeff grinned. "Take it easy, man."

I got to my feet and clumped through the front door, close behind him. A naked bulb hung from the ceiling illuminating the hall. Cigarettes and marijuana butts, empty beer bottles and candy wrappers littered the floor. Holes had been kicked in the walls, broken plaster hung from the ceiling. It stank as though rats had died behind the walls. The stairs were gullied and old. He'd hear everything I did, every step I took. I decided to make him my ally.

"Hey, pal, you wanta give me a hand up the stairs? Last time I went up I fell down and woke the whole house up and my old lady raised hell with me. She didn't talk to me for a whole week."

"How lucky can you get?"

I moved toward him, my hand out. "Come on, pal. Give me a little hand up the stairs."

He was big and nattily attired. He stepped back as though I were going to soil his clothing. "Help yourself up," he said. He began climbing the stairs.

I lurched after him. "People don't give a shit. Nobody gives a shit about anybody."

He turned his head. "You're fuckin' right, man."

"You're a wise guy. Don't give a shit about anybody. Huh? Well, you'll get yours."

He continued upward, ignoring me. I clutched the banister and threw my feet out noisily. He'd accepted a drunk as part of the package. The neighborhood called for guys falling down stairs. It fit. He had nothing to fear from a guy who was bagged.

His destination was an apartment on the third floor. Light shone through a hole where the lock should have been. He rapped three times and called, "Matty." When he turned and saw me, I reeled from wall to wall and crashed down against a door. He grinned and went in.

The door I had bumped opened suddenly. There was a thin, red-faced woman in an Indian-design flannel bathrobe. Her face was damp with perspiration. Her scarlet hair hung limply. She glared at me. "What the hell do you think you're doing?"

"Sorry," I mumbled. "I musta got the wrong number. I'm looking for my wife."

"Well, now goddammit, do I look like your wife?"

"Nobody looks like my wife." I gave her a quick imitation of a crying jag. "I love her, and I can't find her."

She said, "Shit. You're never going to find her." Her laugh was evil. "You ain't ever going to find her because she's hiding from you."

"She ain't, she ain't."

"Yes, she is," she said, and slammed the door shut. I crawled away and sat huddled against the wall in drunken posture.

The boyfriend came out of the apartment and wordlessly passed me by. He went down. From a window at the end of the hall I saw him drive off. I went over to Matty's apartment, rapped on the door and got no reply. Music came from behind the door. I rapped again and got no response. I turned the doorknob and pushed. The door was held by a chain. A little maneuvering with a piece of wire released the chain lock and the door swung open. I was in a living room. There was the after-smell of cooked heroin. There were three brown paper bags overflowing with garbage, waiting for someone to remove them along with a broken fish bowl and three dead goldfish on the floor. Against the wall there was a couch. Springs protruded where it had once smoldered. I had a bad feeling about the apartment and Henri Doran's daughter.

I removed my gun from its holster and went into the bedroom. A young girl in stained brassiere and panties sat on the edge of the bed with her arms hugging her body. She rocked and stared off into space. Her thighs and arms were covered with hit marks.

My presence didn't startle her. She smiled at me. "What you doing here, man?"

I took a chance and said, "Tom sent me up."

She giggled. "He didn't tell me he was sending anybody up tonight, but if he sent you . . . then it's all right with me. Anything Tom wants is okay with me. Tommy takes care of me, and what he wants he gets. Did he tell you how much it was?"

"I forgot."

"It's twenty-five, but I usually get a tip for myself." She giggled. "I take care of you real good if I know there's a little extra for myself." She stretched out and patted the mattress next to her and giggled again. "Over here and bring your money. We got to take care of the man. The man who takes care of. . . ." She fell onto the bed and asleep in the middle of what she was going to say.

I walked away and glanced back at her from the other room. I was sick and caught up in pity for her. I gagged with the stench of garbage.

Zeff was pimping her off. She was hooked, and he was her supplier. He was killing her. I was afraid for Henri Doran's daughter. If Zeff had her on junk, it could already be too late. I felt sad for Henri Doran. I found a telephone and called him and told him that I wanted to come over.

"Is anything wrong?" he asked in a concerned tone.

"It's going to be all right. I'll be right over," I said and hung up.

He answered the door when I rang. We spoke in the living room. He drew a deep breath as though steeling himself. "What is it, Mr. Toma?"

He listened and interrupted once to say, "Dear God." He was ashen when I'd finished. He stood in an attitude of total weariness. He glanced at a photograph of his dead wife and whispered, "Marie, what can I do?" His eyes filled with tears, and I turned away in the awkward silence that followed. "Help me, help me, Mr. Toma."

I stood there like a fool, trying for the proper words. I didn't have them. "When does he usually bring her home?"

"One, one thirty. In an about an hour or two."

I looked directly at him. "Henri, do you know if she takes drugs?"

Sudden bewilderment covered his face. "What are you saying?" he said, his voice choked with emotion. "That my daughter, my daughter. . . . You think my daughter is taking drugs?"

"Please, Mr. Doran. Has she been acting strangely, anything out of the ordinary?"

"I don't know."

"You're her father. You'd have to know."

"I don't. She seemed perfectly all right. There was an argument when I said that I didn't like the young man she was seeing. That upset her. Other than that. . . ." He shook his head in bewilderment.

"I want to look at her bedroom, at her personal belongings."

"Yes, of course. I'll show you." He led me to it.

I removed a drawer and dumped it on her bed.

"She won't like it," Doran said quietly.

"Mr. Doran, I have children too. Sometimes you have to do what they don't like."

"Yes, of course," he said. He helped.

The room looked as though it had been hit by a cyclone. When it seemed that there was nothing there, I found a pillbox buried beneath a stack of magazines. I showed them to him.

"What are they?" he said.

"Purple hearts and rainbows. They're amphetamines and barbiturates."

A tear broke loose and ran down to the corner of his mouth. He was trembling. He excused himself and began to walk from the room.

"Stay here. Help me put all this back the way we found it," I said. "I want you to help me."

When we had finished, he said, "What can I do?"

"Now you do nothing. You say nothing to her."

"But I can't let her continue."

"She isn't going to," I said. I stood up. I was leaving. "I'll see you tomorrow."

I went and got back to my car and waited for an hour until Zeff dropped Doran's daughter off. He left with me on his tail. In the city I managed to keep a few cars between us. He slowed perceptively when he drew near police patrol cars. I imagined that he had something to hide. It was almost two in the morning. The late hour wouldn't prevent him from making another call. Prostitutes work all hours of the night, and my thought was that he had a string. It figured that he was easing Doran's daughter in with pills. She might already be in. I had no way of knowing. The man who eases a girl into the "life" by getting her on drugs is the lowest animal. I've seen the bottom of the barrel, and it's where he is.

He got on the Garden State Parkway, and I put on speed. The Valiant wasn't any match for the Cadillac on a straightaway. I've taken it up to a hundred, but it was hairy. It would be much more comfortable for the Cadillac.

He was looking for a tail. I sensed it. He reduced speed and then put it on again. His objective was to ride the parkway without anyone near him. At the slow speeds passing him could be extremely hazardous. If I passed an exit, there'd be nothing to prevent him from turning off. I'd lose him. He had to be followed from behind. I didn't like it. He pulled another cute trick. Unexpectedly he slowed and pulled up on the grass.

There were two choices. I could pull up on the grass behind him. If I approached his car with drawn gun, there would be a confrontation. I assumed that he was armed. The second choice was less risky. I drove around a bend in the road and pulled in between a cluster of trees with the engine running. Traffic was all one-way. He'd have to pass me. I got out of the car and walked back until I could see him parked. The Cadillac was leaving the grass, burning rubber on the asphalt.

I ran toward my car as a white streak went by. I got it back on the parkway and floored it. He was slowed by a cluster of cars. I pulled up to him at 90. On the straightaway he was going to lose me. I had no choice. I pulled alongside and hit the siren. I caught a glimpse of his face. He cut the wheel toward me, and the Valiant swerved crazily and almost left the road when I tried to avoid him.

He found a space between two cars and shot through, and I was right on his tail. I stayed with him at 100 while the car threatened to shake apart. I had it flat out. He pulled away. He was racing for his life. He lost the race on a turn. He took it too wide and never came out of it. Centrifugal force took him off the road. I estimated his speed at about 120. He sideswiped a sturdy tree with the sound of a cannon, wrapped around it and bounced end over end, twice, and exploded into flames.

I stopped and went back. Cars were stopping all around. People ran toward the flaming wreckage. It was a torch, a blazing coffin that nobody would ever walk away from. I left when the state police arrived and began foaming what was left of the Cadillac. A small quantity of heroin and some charred glassine envelopes were found.

I went back and told Henri Doran and his daughter what had happened. Everything, including her involvement with Zeff, the pills she was taking, was brought out into the open. She denied any knowledge of Zeff's real background, and I believed her. What Zeff had in mind brought her back down to earth with a resounding crash. It opened her eyes. She was intelligent enough to realize that Zeff had a few unsavory plans for her. She straightened herself out, and Henri Doran felt indebted to me.

When I asked to do my thing in his restaurant, he came through.

The guy who came in was big, broad across the shoulders, with salt and pepper hair slicked back. He spoke to one of the headwaiters and specified that he wanted one of my tables. It was an order. He wore an impeccably tailored black silk suit; his hands were manicured, the heavy cuff links were solid gold. He studied the menu with the aid of horn-rimmed glasses, handed it back to me and said, "Scotch on the rocks, the house dressing on my salad and rare prime ribs with a baked potato."

I said, "Thank you."

He said, "Toma, make sure the roast beef is rare."

I ignored the "Toma." Disguised, while out on the street, I'd schooled myself never to turn around if somebody suspected and was testing.

I said, "Yes, sir, I'll see to it."

He gave me a steady, direct gaze. He wasn't testing my disguise. He knew it was me. "What time do you finish up here, Toma?"

"Toma? I think you're making a mistake. Do I know you?"

"I know you."

"From where?"

"Let's not play games. You know the Deli on the triangle near your home? We picked you up there and followed you as far as the Howard Johnson. We dropped you, and we put another tag on you, two cars this time. On the parkway one stayed back. At the toll, the rear car took over."

"It sounds like an elaborate plan."

"It was. You're playing your own game. You haven't been checking in at the precinct. When we want to find a man, we can find him." He laughed. He was enjoying himself. His authority was in the way he sat. Every nuance told me that he felt in full control.

"You found me. What do you want?"

"A pleasant talk."

"Now, or after the prime rib?"

"I'm in no rush, and you're not going anywhere. Why don't you have coffee with me?"

"I'm working."

"You're through here. If you continue to work here, you'll work as a waiter and not as an undercover cop."

He had a point. I went off and put his order in. Henri studied him through a circular window in the kitchen's swinging door. "That's Joe Jamison. He's been here before. He's a racket guy."

I didn't know him. "And?"

"I've seen him with John Ambruso. They come in about twice a month."

I knew John Ambruso. "Anybody else with them?"

"No. It's just the two of them. They sit like they're talking business. I've got a feeling that some of the information you pick up here you've already used against them."

He'd hit it on the head. "I'll be through here tonight."

"Yes," Henri said. "That might be wise. Sooner or later they might want to learn who hired you."

"They don't have any reason to come to you, and even if they did, you don't even know me. There isn't any way that they can tie us together. You understand?"

"Of course."

"Are you frightened?"

"No. I trust you. I believe what you've told me."

"Good," I said. I finished up two tables and then brought Jamison his check. "Everything all right?"

"Fine. The roast beef was excellent."

I brought the check up front and returned and sat down with coffee. "Very good coffee here," I said.

He wanted to talk, and I let him. "Toma, you've been very busy here. You busted a bank and a drop. Word gets around. Very good. You're doing a fine job." There was no anger in his tone.

"Thank you," I said. He had a lot more to say, and I waited for him.

"I'm a man who doesn't like to see talent wasted. Now you've got a lot of talent, and you're wasting it as a cop."

"I'm flattered. What have you got in mind for me?"

"You know Big John. He's a nice guy, and he's your own kind. Not only that, but he told me that his father and your father came from the same town in Italy."

"No kidding. I didn't know that."

"Yeah, it's true. Anyway, Big John is putting up some nice apartment houses in Atlantic City and in Trenton, and he's bought land for a development in Margate. He's helping to improve the area, and he's providing people with places to live."

"Good for him. He sounds like a fine, civic-minded citizen,

but he doesn't sound like the Big John that I knew. Are you sure
we're talking about the same guy? They guy I remember is
involved in the rackets."

He took a slow breath. "Come on, Toma. I came here to talk.
I've got a business proposition."

"Okay. Why don't you put it in plain talk?"

He nodded. "Sure. I'll get right to it. But first let's talk about
you for a minute. People are always going to gamble. So you're
going around busting places, and what does it all mean?
Nothing."

"Some of those places belong to Big John?"

He gave me a pained look. "I didn't say that. What I'm
leading up to is that you're wasting your time. You're not going
to change anything. You're not going to be with the police the
rest of your life anyway. A man has to look to the future."

"That's true."

He nodded. "So here's what Big John has got in mind. He has
a lot of money tied up in investments, business, legitimate
businesses. He needs good people who will work for him,
dependable people."

"Work for him? How?"

He smiled. "I understand your apprehension. You'd have to
leave the police. He's offering you a job. Whatever you're
making, he'll pay you double. Of course, you'll have to leave the
police."

"I don't think so."

He spread his hands in a friendly gesture. "Why would you
want to stay with the police?"

"I'm a cop. I like cops, and I like being a cop."

"Toma, I don't mean any offense by what I'm going to say.
Before we consider hiring a man, we investigate him. We have
a lot of people telling us things. We know things about you. You

don't have any money to talk about. You're running around making speeches about narcotics, telling people how bad it is, and you're not even getting paid for it. You have to be for yourself, Toma. You get nothing by being for the whole world, nothing. What are you trying to prove?"

"I'm not sure. Maybe that there's a difference between myself and Big John."

"That could be, but what you do isn't going to hurt Big John. Maybe you send a few of his people to jail. So what? Nothing stops. Things go on just the same. A place gets closed up, and another one opens. That's the way of the world. You don't hurt powerful people. I know it, and you know it too. You've been a cop a long time. What did it ever get you?"

I laughed. "Sometimes I wonder. I met some good people. A little purpose to my life. Who knows? A little respect?"

"What are you going to buy with respect? A guy like you makes twelve thousand dollars a year. You're not going to set the world on fire with that figure. And for that kind of money you take a lot of wild chances. You're playing with percentages. Sooner or later your luck will run out."

"Are you threatening me?"

"Not me. I'm just telling you the way it is. I'm here to offer you a job, and I'm trying to show you all sides. The way I see it, sooner or later you're going to give somebody a headache."

"You?"

He laughed aloud. "Not us. We survive because we're strong. You can't hurt us. I'm talking about an organization that isn't as strong in the money department. Break some of their banks and send some of their top men away, and you can put them in a bad business position. These are the people I'd worry about if I were you."

"I see. You're talking to me because you're concerned about

somebody else giving me a hard time. What about these people? Who are they? What do you think they'd do?"

"I don't know them. Listen, how can you tell what anybody is going to do? I know guys who will change a man's face for a hundred dollars. That's no money at all. But they'll do it."

"You're telling me to lay off."

"No, I'm not. I'm offering you a job with Big John. You're no threat to us. We genuinely feel that you can be an asset to us. We've got some friends at the city, county and state level. We've got a lot of power. You could be a big man with us. You know people, you could talk to them."

"You'd want me to be a middleman, sort of a liaison man, a public relations man."

He smiled. "You understand. I knew you would. What do you say?"

I understood it perfectly. "Here's the way I see it. You say one thing, and you mean something else. You're not talking about a small operator that I can hurt. You're talking about yourselves."

Jamison sighed. "You're wrong."

"You figure that if you've got an ex-cop on your payroll that knows how you operate, he'll be able to wise you up on how to protect yourselves."

"Be smart, Toma. It's a good job with good money."

I was tired. My back ached, and my feet hurt from waiting on tables. I was tired of Jamison's bullshit. "Tell Big John it's like this. We forget that business about us both being Italian. That means nothing to me. He's not my kind of *paisan*. The Italians I know are good people. They raise fine, decent families. They're honest and hardworking, and they break their ass just like everybody else to keep a roof over their heads. And once in a while they listen to a lot of crap because of a bum like

Ambruso. I don't like that. You tell him he's into junk and he's bankrolling it with dirty money. That makes him a murderer. I don't care if he's Italian, Greek, Jewish, Swedish, or green, black, tan, white or orange. If he thinks that he's going to murder people without people trying to stop him, then he's mistaken."

Jamison was pale with anger. "You take big chances, Toma."

"You tell Big John that if I ever catch him wrong, I'll break him. Tell that bum you work for that I don't consider him civilized.

CHAPTER SEVENTEEN

It was a busy week for the Bureau of Investigation. Casatelli was busted by a squad of detectives for loan sharking and operating a gambling ring. He'd given his wife a rough time. It would have given me a little more satisfaction if I had been in on the arrest. It got him a five-year jail sentence.

On Tuesday night I was on a gambling detail when I saw a prostitute solicit a guy on the street. She took him to an abandoned building. I followed out of habit, I think. I found them stark naked in a doorless apartment. He offered some resistance, and the girl took advantage of the opportunity to dart into the hall and out onto the street. I gave chase. She ran swiftly. Circumstances were not conducive for pursuit. It was early evening in the middle of July. People sat on stoops and milled about, seeking a breath of air. The girl was black, nude and running for her life with a white man chasing her through a black area. She was imaginative. In the midst of her flight she began yelling, "Help! Help! Rape! Rape!"

I said, "What the hell, is she crazy?" I detected that others had joined the chase. A fast backward glance revealed about fifty black guys closing in fast and shouting ugly words with ugly meanings.

I was in the wrong place at the wrong time. It wasn't a place for me. It was suitable for some of my enemies. I hit the brakes, U-turned and flew back in the direction whence I had come, utilizing a little broken-field running. I avoided a tackle and sprinted toward the car a block away, spurred on by threats. An 80-mile-an-hour wind wouldn't have overtaken me. The Valiant lurched out of there in the midst of a small angry black army raining fists on the roof. A man could get killed out there. I went home and soaked in a hot tub and played stereophonic music.

In the morning I was summoned by Inspector Irving J. Moore. He'd been called in by the bureau to revitalize its attack on gambling, which had fallen off. Moore was a good police officer with a well-earned reputation. He was a thick-chested, affable man, quick to smile and give credit for a job well done and equally quick to disapprove when the work wasn't done properly. He stated what he wanted in blunt fashion. "The bureau isn't coming up with its quota of arrests in gambling." He studied me. "I know who you are and how you operate. You're a maverick, but you produce. That's all I can ask of a man. I'm not giving you a definite assignment. Handle it any way you like. I want you to put a dent in gambling. I'm relying on you for it."

I said, "Okay," and went to work.

By noon I'd latched onto a pickup man. I tagged him as he went into a notions store and then lost him in a restaurant. He went in and didn't come out again. I waited fifteen minutes, went in, and he was gone. He could have departed by a rear exit door.

Back on the street I walked and went over what had happened. I'd followed a guy that I'd spotted as a pickup man. I was sure of it. He was about five ten, husky, dark-haired and he wore a sport shirt and slacks. One man had left the restaurant. He was built the same, but his hair was lighter and he wore work clothes and carried refrigeration testing equipment.

I thought of him. It couldn't have been the same man, and yet there was something similar in his walk. It gave me something to think about for the rest of the day.

At eleven on the following morning, I picked him up again where I had first seen him. I detected a wig. He was doing my thing. He was using disguises. He went into the restaurant as a mechanic and came out with a briefcase and attired in a lightweight business suit. He was very careful. He rode a bus for ten blocks, then transferred to a taxi heading north. The taxi stopped in the middle of a block and he transferred to a taxi going in the other direction. I lost him.

He repeated the pattern on the next day, using different disguises. On the fourth day I was ready for him. I borrowed a taxi from a fleet owner I know. I tailed him on the bus, and when he stopped and climbed into a cab, I drove past him and tailed him from up front. When we drew near the block where he had switched cabs, I was well ahead. I turned back so that I was facing his taxi, waiting for him. He hailed me and climbed in.

"Where to?" I said.

He gave me an address. I drove him there, walked in behind him and busted him and two guys in an apartment.

Three days later Patty was manhandled on a crowded bus

during the rush hour by two hoods as she stood laden with packages. One of them moved next to her and said, "You're Patty Toma, right? I'd know you in a minute. I'm an old buddy of Dave's." The other man put his hand on her waist. As she protested, he said, "Keep your mouth shut. Make some noise and you'll never walk off this thing."

The other man said, "How are the kids? You've got Jimmy, right? That's the kid who pitches baseball. Yeah, he's a nice kid. Then there's Patty Anne and Donna and Janice. All nice kids. Jimmy goes to the school over on Broadhurst, right? We know he leaves by the side entrance at two o'clock."

They pawed until she began to bawl. When she dropped her packages, they knelt beside her. One of them held her chin and kissed her forehead. "So long, Patty. Give Dave a message. Tell him he's working too hard. He can get sick like that. Tell him to take it easy."

I went home as soon as she called. The kids were all there except Jimmy. He usually came directly home after school. On that day he wasn't there. I had police out looking for him.

I tried to reassure Patty. "They won't do anything to him. I know them. They're trying to throw a scare."

She didn't answer.

"I'm sorry, Patty. What I do outside isn't supposed to touch my family."

"Isn't it?" she asked sharply. "I don't see any written guarantee. When we lived in the ghetto, they slashed your tires and threw rocks through our windows because you wouldn't stop!"

"I'm sorry." I had no answer for her.

A radio car brought my son home. He'd gone to visit one of his friends. My wife held onto him and cried.

Moore called me into his office and got right down to what he had to say. "I want you off it for a while. No more gambling details. You've had enough. They're not playing games with you anymore."

"Who is the 'they' you're talking about?"

"Does it really matter? Does it make any difference who they are? You've got nine thousand arrests. Who knows who it could be? It could be some jerk you arrested two months ago."

"It could be Ambruso."

"Yeah, it could. And it could also be this guy you booked who was using disguises. It could even be Casatelli. I know he's in jail, but it could be that some of his guys are operating again."

I said, "They went after my family. They touched my wife."

Moore looked uncomfortable. He looked away for a minute, then turned back. "You're vulnerable. They know who you are, where you live, what your car looks like, where you park and the route you travel coming to the precinct." He paused. "You've got a family." He pointed. "You're off this case. If anything happens, I don't want it on my head."

"They went after my family."

"Did you hear what I said? You're off. Am I getting through to you, Toma?"

I said nothing. I knew that he was right.

"I'll have some men keep an eye on your family," he said. In a softer tone, "I'm sorry, Dave."

I went out and drove through the ghetto. I was worried about my family. My head throbbed with it. The consequences involved, if I continued to go after gambling, could be disastrous. If there was any fear for myself, my anger wiped it out. Some apprehension came from it. I found myself checking the mirror for a possible tag.

On South Orange Avenue a guy in front of me in a black Pontiac jumped the light. It wasn't important. He wasn't running from anything. He parked midway down the block. Jumping the light had merely been an unthinking act. He hadn't done it deliberately in the interests of speed. He'd committed a small traffic violation. So what?

A policeman observes because it's his job. It becomes instinctive. I parked and watched him as he went into an apartment building and came out carrying a small package. He left and I tagged him for six stops. The action was identical. He was picking up apartment houses and small stores. I had a pickup man in my sights. I used five disguises to ride his tail.

I hadn't forgotten what Moore had told me. I'd noted each address. Others could follow them up.

He stopped at a bar, and I went in and observed a woman handing him a small package and some money.

His next stop was a whorehouse. There was no doubt. A few furtive-looking guys drove up and went into the building. Some others gave it away with an overabundance of studied nonchalance. My pickup man was in there long enough to get some. He was out on the street on his own. I doubted that he'd report it to his boss. What they didn't know wouldn't hurt them. He was grabbing something extra on the company's time.

He left, and I tagged along to East Orange. I wondered about the bordello. It could have been a drop or a bank. More likely it was a place where a guy could get laid. I became more careful. When he parked on Williams Street and began walking, I followed him by car. Perhaps I was being too careful. I've known them to use three and four cars when they suspect a tail. They'll walk along for two blocks while you're following on foot and suddenly take off in another car that's parked up ahead waiting for them. They're gone by the time you get back to your car to pursue.

I followed by car and distributed telephone directories, running from one side of the street to the other. He suspected nothing when I followed him into an apartment building.

From a stair landing above I observed him rapping on a door. He entered. I went down, listened, heard telephones ringing and went back to the landing again to wait. Fifteen minutes went by, and a blonde woman carrying a shopping bag came out. I guessed her name was Ms. Bookmaker. I left the pickup man and followed her. She was nicer. She drove her red Cadillac convertible with confidence, with the top down, radio blasting. She was on home ground, destination Baker's Tavern on Jackson Avenue in Jersey City. I double-parked and observed. The doors were open. She went into the tavern and right out the back door with the shopping bags.

I circled the block like a wild man, against a one-way street, parked and ran through a guy's backyard. From behind a wooden fence I saw the blonde hand the shopping bag to two controllers. She was the dropman. She was finished. She left and went back into the bar.

The building adjacent to the bar extended past it for about twenty feet. At street level it was the rear of the restaurant. One of the controllers took the shopping bag and dropped it into a black metal exhaust at the rear of the restaurant. Above the restaurant there was a single apartment that ran the full length of the structure. The controllers went into the tavern and kept the blonde company. When one left, I followed him home. For the day I had license numbers, a pickup man, a dropman, seven stops and a restaurant that could be a bank.

It had been a busy day. I went back and told it all to Moore.

He took a deep breath. "I told you that you were off the case and off all special-detail gambling."

"I didn't look for it. It was there in front of me, the whole run, from Newark, to East Orange to Jersey City."

"East Orange and Jersey City are out of your jurisdiction. You're bouncing all over the lot."

"It's a big operation. I know it."

"They're out there looking for you, Toma."

"It's going to take me weeks. They'll never know that I'm on it."

"I'll give you a few more men."

"I don't want any."

"You don't make any sense."

"I've got a better shot without them. Let me play it my way, and I'll get you the top man."

"And they'll pin it on you if you do. There are seven stops. We could set up on all that and bust them."

"You've got a chance at the big man, at breaking the operation if this outfit is as big as I think it is."

"Listen, he picks up at seven places. You've seen them. It would be sure. The shot at the big man is a gamble."

"Everything is a gamble. What have you got the other way, Inspector? We're in a city where all the people see are creeps and nobody's getting busted. Cops chasing guys who are shooting dollar craps in an alley. What have we got here? If we don't bust the big man, we lose. He takes the whole city over. He gets fat. He's feeding off people who live with rats. Ask a kid in the ghetto if he would like to be a cop, and he'll look at you as though you're crazy. He wants to grow up to be a button man or a lieutenant or a hit man in the organization. He thinks the big man is something special, out of the ordinary and that he can't be touched by the law."

Moore gave me a thoughtful glance. "In a lot of ways he is. He surrounds himself with layers of protection. It's tough to reach him. It isn't that easy, Toma."

"Nobody says it's easy."

"He didn't get to the top of the heap by being a dummy."

278

"Wrong. He is a dummy, and you can get to him. You can cut right through all that insulation that's shielding him."

"How?"

"You follow the action from the beginning, the player, the pickup man, the drop, the bank. Take it right down the line. It has to lead to the bank."

"What makes you think he's there? What makes you so sure?"

"Money."

"Money?"

"That's it. There aren't any checks. People spend money when they gamble with bookmakers. Somebody has to count it. How many people can he trust when it comes to counting a ton of loose money? In nine cases out of ten he's sitting right on the bank himself. It's a cash business because it has to be. It's the only way he can do business. He can't issue a check when somebody hits a number for fifteen hundred dollars. How is he going to explain a canceled check? He pays off in cash, and he only accepts cash. And the cash has to leave a trail. People have to move it, carry it, deliver it. They're out on the street, jumpy, moving it, hiding it, carrying it, and they can be seen. They're visible."

"You really believe that. . . ."

"I know it. They think they're safe because they deal in cash. Cash is a giveaway. I've been saying it for years, but I haven't been able to sell it to anybody."

He studied my face for a while. "I buy it. It makes sense." He got up and walked around his office and got back to me. "You don't try to break this on your own. All right, you want to do the surveillance on your own, that's okay. But when it comes to the actual bust, you let me know. You go in with plenty of help. I like to sleep nights."

I said, "Inspector, it's a pleasure doing business with you." It was. I began to leave. "I'd appreciate it if somebody would keep an eye on my family."

He was looking at some reports on his desk. Without looking up he said, "I've already assigned more men in addition to those who are there."

I called my wife and told her that I'd be late and then went back to all locations where the pickup man had been. I got as much of the layout as was possible in one night. How many doors, exits, types of locks and alarm systems. It was midnight when I got home. I fell into bed, exhausted.

In the morning I visited Baker's Tavern in Jersey City, as a telephone repairman, Good Humor man, derelict, Chicano, house painter, priest and doctor, spreading a warning about an epidemic of venereal disease.

The controllers had a busy day dropping play into the restaurant's exhaust next door. The restaurant was my next step. I got in as a Health inspector. I ate veal and noodles in the kitchen and checked for violations and found none. There was a locked door at the far end of the kitchen. I pointed and said, "Open it."

The boss shrugged. "Hey, what do you want? We run a clean place. It's an old storeroom with an old potbellied stove in it, that's all."

"I have to see it."

He unlocked the door and I saw the stove with the black metal exhaust that led outside the building and received the gambling play. The room itself was little more than a closet. The play had to be moved from there and counted elsewhere. But where? I couldn't hang around the kitchen all day waiting for someone to take the money from the stove.

A roof on a building overlooking the restaurant kitchen became my vantage point. I went up a ladder in coveralls and hammered roof shingles down. A guy with a cigar stuck his head out of a window. "Hey, what are you doing banging on the roof?"

"You got a homeowner's policy on this house?"

"Yeah, so?"

"So the insurance company told me to come down and fix all the loose shingles."

"They expecting a storm or something?"

"Who knows? It doesn't cost you anything."

"That's good." The window slammed shut.

The view into the kitchen was good. A man dressed as a kitchen helper went to the potbellied stove and came out with a canvas bag. He walked to a big exhaust vent over the kitchen stove, threw a switch and shoved the bag up into the duct. It disappeared, sucked up into the ductwork.

The ductwork led up into the ceiling. The apartment had to be the destination of the canvas bag. I descended my ladder, lowered it to the ground and placed it flat against the building foundation. My goal was to take a gander at the apartment over the restaurant. Somebody running a bank wasn't going to open doors readily.

It seemed a difficult problem, but it turned out to be relatively simple. I returned that evening and under cover of darkness retrieved my ladder and stealthily carried it into the backyard behind the tavern. One window was lighted in the apartment. A screen door slammed at the rear of the tavern. I crouched behind stacked beer kegs. A man came out, set an empty soda bottle case down and went back inside.

I raised the ladder and rested it as quietly as I could against the outside wall of the apartment. I made my way up and took a careful look. There was no one around. It was a living room, very expensively furnished, marble end tables and elegant couches. Paintings hung on the walls. The living room didn't belong on Jackson Avenue in Jersey City in an upstairs apartment above a restaurant. It was more like a Hollywood set.

A man came into the room. I stood frozen. I had a glimpse of him full face before I ducked down. I had seen Big John Ambruso. I couldn't have been mistaken. I lowered the ladder very carefully and hastened away in the darkness. I hoisted the ladder over a fence and deposited it in a neighboring backyard. I didn't want it found near Ambruso's apartment in the morning.

I called Moore and told him what I'd seen. "Ambruso is sitting right on the bank. It looks like a dive from the outside; but inside it's a palace."

Moore said, "It figures for a guy like Ambruso."

"You warned me about trying to break this thing on my own. I'm going to need all the official help I can get."

"It's going to take the state police and the prosecutor's office for permission for you to go into East Orange and Jersey City. Come on down. It's going to be a busy evening. I'll get some people in here. We've got some heavy planning to do."

It took a few days to set it up.

The raid encompassed Newark, East Orange and Jersey City. They were hit simultaneously. It broke a $20,000,000-a-year operation and made front-page headlines. It was the largest gambling bust in the state's history.

Ambruso was sent up to keep Casatelli company. You don't always get the big guy, but he can be busted. He's no superman. He's not above the law. Nobody is. I was never able to learn whether it was his men on the bus with Patty.

I consider myself fortunate. I live in a good country and I have faith in it. I have faith in the people. The people are the country, and the people are beautiful. We are of hardy stock. We survive, and we endure. I'm proud of my family, my wife, Patty, and our children. I belong to another family too, a family of police officers, perhaps as a maverick. If I had the choice of doing it all over again, it would be in the role of a police officer. There were rewards. I know addicts who kicked it and stayed clean. I hope I've been instrumental in that to some small degree and in preventing others from becoming drug-addicted. I believe in dignity for all people. I'm grateful for the thousands of letters I've received from children. I've received many awards.

From the Police Benevolent Association there was a plaque:

> David Toma—A crusader in the fight to maintain the humane qualities of man in the theater of crime.

I'd like to be remembered that way.

DATE DUE

NOV 19, 2002				
IEL 920365				
4/1/13				